Vida

Vida

Alma Luz Villanueva

*To see directly the wonder of the order
and the chaos of the Universe
would be extraordinary.*

– Don Juan, in *Magical Passes*,
by Carlos Castañeda

San Antonio, Texas
2002

Vida © 2002 by Alma Luz Villanueva

ISBN: 0-930324-66-8

Wings Press
627 E. Guenther
San Antonio, Texas 78210
(210) 271-7805

On-line catalogue and ordering:
www.wingspress.com

Villanueva, Alma, 1944 -
Vida / Alma Luz Villanueva
    p.   cm.
ISBN   0-930324-66-8   (non acidic paper)
1. Mexican American women – poetry. 1. Title.
2001

The publication of *Vida* is supported in part
by a grant from the National Endowment for the Arts.

Some the poems in *Vida* have appeared previously
in to following publications:
Fourteen Hills (*San Francisco State University Review*, Fall 1996);
Letters to My Father, Things I Meant to Tell You, anthology (Story Line
Press, Spring 2001); *Caprice Review* (Spring 1998); She Rises Like the
Sun, anthology (Crossing Press, 1990); *MS. Magazine* (May/June
1995); *Caprice Review* (Fall 1999); *Caprice Review* (Spring 2000).
Poetry from this collection was also included in *The Best American
Poetry, 1996*.

The publisher wishes to thank Oisín Mabry for editorial assistance.

CONTENTS

To all my ancestors past, present, the future

WILD ROOT

Wild Root

I break a plant, heavy
with blossoms and growth —
I'm sad as though someone's
died — I take it to a healer,
a young woman — I follow
her through huge deserted
rooms where she transplants
the roots in fertile soil —
I see the Grand Canyon
and pause to watch it, carefully,
as it crumbles — centuries
pass — the plant and I live
in the root — in the wild
wild root.

Dream, December 1993

Vida

My aunt sinks into her
own bones, working hard

to find her way to the center
of the Earth, to the center

of her Self (why was she born...
to weep, laugh, live,

why) — she follows a trail
of smoke that sings her

life, the smoke she breathed
in her mother's womb —

heart-fire, blood-fire,
star-fire, desire's only

song: TO LIVE FOREVER.

⚭ ⚭

She tosses her head, closes
her eyes, calls her mother's

name; she searches for the
Source; the smoke burns

her lungs, waters her eyes,
as it swirls the room

(ancestors swirl sage, eucalyptus —
they chant, "To the Center,

Ruth, to the Center, Ruth,
of the Earth's desires" —)

The unspeakable act of leaving
the body behind, gift

to the planet, follow
the smoke to the origin

of fire (why why why),
leave your body behind.

Now, *you are the smoke*
trailing back to the

ancient, newly born
fire, and you sing

your own sweet song
as you trail back,

swirling, unborn, undead,
you remember (O you re

member, pues, si, you re
member, otra vez, you re

member, swirling, free of
the Earth, you remember) why,

O Chispa   Lumbre   Luz.
Vida.

∞ ∞

My aunt tells me:
"You shoot for the stars,

and you get there, yes,
you do." You too,

tía, you too.

> *A mi tía, Ruth Villanueva Mendolla,*
> *to her death/transformation,*
> *August 7, 1994*

People of the Spiral (Anasazi Ruins)

We follow the ruins,
the stones set into the earth,
where the Ancient Ones dreamt,
ate, laughed, wept, gave birth,

left the body for the distant
stars: home: Earth: home.
They knew how they came,
and from where: that Spiral

of stars, so far you fly
until you can't, until the spirit
is willing to leave the body —
only then will the Spiral

pull you: home. They knew
how they came, the Ancient Ones,
and they left. In a meadow,
a smooth green place, smoothed

by centuries of their hands, we enter
it, my son and I, we hear clear
silence and voices in the soft
soft sunlight. The voices

are gentle, a murmur like wind,
women, children, men, then silence,
then voices, soft laughter,
a child's brief cry. A rabbit

appears to greet us, without any
fear, she sits in our company,
reminding me who we are, people
of the Spiral: home.

"Do not be fooled," she murmurs,
"by the ruins of civilization,
I remember you, how you smoothed
this earth, how you ate my

flesh, how you treasured my
skin for warmth and beauty,
how you loved me, sang songs
to me, I remember you both..."

Then her ears stiffen as the
others approach, their footsteps,
their scent unfamiliar. And she's
gone. I crush sage between my

fingers, the familiar scent
of life here
so long ago,
today.

> *On Navaho land, May 1995,*
> *where Spirits and Animals*
> *rise up and speak,*
> *and coyotes call, sing,*
> *call in the morning hills,*
> *trout gather in groups, leap*
> *for the new*
> *Sun.*

Weighing My Father's Soul

to Whitey, born January 21, 1911

Like birdsong beginning inside the egg.

– Rumi

1.

You come to me at sunset, on your birth day;
you, my father, 80 miles away, leaving, oh leaving,
your body (you are not the father of my body,
you are the father of my soul). Your soul comes to

me, I feel it floating in the air, I breathe it in,
tell stories: He fed me when I was 12 and hungry,
a wild tomboy kid, called me Pocahontas when I refused
to say my name, my grandmother gone, now it was his

turn. He gave me all his money when he drank on
payday (he worked the manholes of San Francisco),
told me not to give it back, even if he asked,
begged, demanded, until Monday morning, so

I hid it in a can, in the dark, in the cobwebbed
basement. Monday, I gave every dollar back. In
return, $20 for the movies, Playland at the Beach,
new tennis shoes, white socks, my first AAA bra.

I stole his Kools, smoked them one by one in the
back row of the movies on Mission Street with
friends, and when boys tried to sit next to me
I'd threaten them with my fists or a burning

cigarette. He gave me his old wool army jackets
(which I loved), loaned me his
fishing tackle, pole and reel.
This stranger who sometimes drank

too much and told me stories of his life
(how he ran away from home at 12,
hopped the rails from Texas to Los Angeles,
leaving his younger brothers and sisters

behind to be beaten; he threw rations to the
hungry children that ran after the jeeps in
World War II: "I ain't never seen kids that
hungry, that kind of hunger's a crime, some

a them carryin' a baby as big as themselves . . ."
Worked in a burlesque house, the women
let him sleep there, safe, each woman
his dead mother, sold papers on the

corner, ran errands for everyone, the
lively, smart-talking, wiry, towheaded
kid nick-named Whitey).
This generous whiskey in the stomach,

tears in the eyes never falling,
maker of stews, spaghetti, deep-fried
chicken with frozen carrots and peas
baker of cherry cakes and too sweet

pink cherry frosting, with sweeter yet
blood-red cherries on top, their stems
teasing the air: he was,
oh yes, he was

my father.

2.

Pregnant at 14, my daughter at 15,
my first son at 17, he brought
groceries 2 or 3 times a week,
taking the bus out to the Sunnydale

Projects in San Francisco;
taking the bus home at night, he
startled a group of kids closing
in to mug him as he waited for

the bus, offering them a few bucks,
"Kind a cold out here, ain't it, well,
hell, here's a few ta tide ya over." They
became his bodyguards, waiting till the

headlights revealed him standing in the
dark with 5 black teenage boys —
they even stopped taking his few bucks,
just standing and laughing with a white

guy crazy enough to be called Whitey,
and tell them, who treated them like
needy children (which they were, there
in those dangerous streets where women

were raped nightly, men shot, people
beaten up for a few bucks). They took
care of him because he took care of
them the way strangers

had taken care of
him in the city

of the Angels when
he was a child of

12, 13, 14, 15.

3.

There were times I had to stand up
to him, both times he was drunk,
beyond the stage where he told stories,
made stangers laugh, made me laugh,

when his pain became the sheerest
of rage, when he wanted to die,
when he wanted to kill (himself
really), and it made his eyes

glassy, unblinking, fearsome;
a warrior, a soldier without fear,
without any fear, facing the enemy
out there. Then, curses, stumbling,

curses, stumbling, passed out.
Once he demanded entrance, I saw
the unblinking eyes and refused.
He shoved the door hard, striking

my chest. Without thinking, I punched
him in the face. Shock. Disbelief.
He yelled, "Goddamn you!" Stepped forward
to hit me, his face red, unfamiliar, his eyes

so blue they hurt. I stood there. Wouldn't back
down (I could already feel his fist, his large

fist, crush me). Then, he remembered who
I was, still angry, now sad,

"Goddamn stupid kid, I could
kill you, you stupid skinny kid..."
I was 13, I stood my ground for
me, for him, for the tears in

his eyes never falling.

4.

The other time I was a grown woman,
visiting him and Lydia (my birth
mother), with my second son, a teenager,
my third son, a baby. Down from

the mountains, the Sierras, my cabin in
the Plumas National Forest, giving birth
to a son, living with the other, on my
own, as the Goddess gazed at me

daily, nightly, with her fierce
fierce love. And the God, he wept
with sorrow, as well as joy, without
restraint. I was learning to be their

child (me with 4 children). My 15 year old
son, Marc, loved him (as did my 19 year old
son, my 21 year old daughter), and he didn't
want to leave when I said, "Meet me at the

car, now," when I saw his unblinking
eyes. Lydia wouldn't leave with me, she

went to her room, locked her door, called
the police to calm him down if necessary

(once a neighbor called them to put him
to bed, him standing in the street in his
underwear, trying to share a drink with
anyone passing by, "Come on and have a drink

with Whitey!") He came to the car to stop me,
cursing, stumbling, sitting next to me, cursing.
I picked up a wrench under my seat for changing
the hubs to 4 wheel drive and held it firmly

in my hand: "If you don't get out, Whitey,
I'll fucking clobber you, I swear it!" Later,
he said he was sorry, quickly, "In front of
the kids'n all," sorry for being the shadow

of the monster he left at 12 (the only
time he ever said he was sorry, to me,
or perhaps anyone). Or how he met
Lydia: she wandered into his apartment,

carrying my baby brother, while he was
drinking with his friends: "That woman
was sittin' on a chicken," he told me
(her office job barely paid the need to

live). "Take the damn chicken and here's
a $40 for the baby, Jesus Christ, I told
that woman," he said laughing.
And that's how their relationship

began, by paying her, but he loved
her, though I know he never told

her; his humor told her, their mutual
vaudeville act: "That woman don't know

her ass from a hole in the ground,
I tell you!" "Shut up, Whitey, you
wouldn't know a hole in the ground if
you fell in it ass first, ha ha!" Who am I

to question 39 years, Goddess? God.

5.

(Weighing the soul together)

The goodness in you was ripe,
full of the sweetest berries,
a rash of thorns; and in your
thick, wild hedge

that came to harvest
for 85 years, so many hungry
wild birds came to feed until
their beaks were stained with

your varied sweetness, the bitter
ones too, and their needy bellies
swelled with your ripeness;
their songs swelled the wind

and carried to the sacred mountains,
to the sacred sea, and the bear,
the coyote, the mountain lion, the
rattler, the wolf, the whale, the seal,

the red-tailed hawk, the fertile fields
between (as well as the deserts), the raven
of your birth, heard your spirit in their songs:
O generous one, O kind one, O suffering one,

your kindnesses outweigh
your cruelties — your gentleness
outweighs your rage — your wonder
outweighs your sorrow.

You weigh less than a tongue —
you weigh less than a breath —
you weigh less than a feather —
you weigh more than your wonder.

You brought the doctor to my bed
when I was 13, when I knew I had
to be a girl, stopped eating, wanted
to die. You brought me soups, juices,

sat in a silence thick with
words never said, but felt, your
presence. You helped me get my first
apartment when I was 16, your constant

supply of groceries, something here,
something there, to tide me over.
At 17, when my second child was born,
in the projects, I was so ill

you stayed for 3 days, taking care
of me, my newborn son, my 2 year old
daughter (their father gone to soldiers);
I could hear you playing with them,

the soothing comfort of your rich
careless laugh. In the 40 years
I have known you, you never said
the words I love you or called

me daughter out loud.
My beak is red, as are my children's.
Your hedge is wild and lush, unpruned.
No words are necessary in this silence

as I feel your heartbeat in the palm of
my hand; I touch your infant's face
(palms to each cheek); your granddaughter
and I change your diaper for the last

time; they lift your body to the gurney
(I hold your knees, the ones you were
born with); I tell the men who will take
your body to the burning: "This is

the most generous, most kind man,
I have ever known, or will probably
ever know." I don't say
I love you or that you are

my father; they understand
this. They know this when I say
(they've wrapped you, plastic/cotton):
"Can I see his face one more time?"

Palms to your old man's face, I whisper,
"I love you, go to the light, I love you,"
and I know I said it for both of us,
and I know you were seeking the light,

father.
The goodness
in you is ripe,
full of creation's

wonder: birth.

6.

In my grandmother's country
(Mexico) where her babies died,
she told me she covered them
with flowers, flowers in water

surrounding them; she sat with them
for 3 days, making sure their spirits
didn't linger, then she let their bodies
go, go into the dark Mexican earth. Then,

on the graves she planted flowers, watered
them, making sure they thrived; each blossom
proof of their rebirth. The spirit.
I see her picking them, smelling them,

taking them home to live in water.
I see the tears in her eyes, the smile
on her young, full mouth. I see her
pregnant with the next one, saying,

"Welcome back, my flower,
welcome back, my soul."
When she left Mexico in her early
thirties, she left nothing behind.

She knew how to grieve the dead,
she knew how to weep their names,
she knew how to breathe them in,
she knew how to dream the spirit,

leaving nothing behind, gathering her
dead in memory, dreams, her
swelling body. I look at
my daughter as we sit by

my father's (her grandfather's)
body; our flowers, the morphine
we fed him, drop by drop (poppies,
hyacinth, iris, roses, birds of

paradise), until he blossomed with
peace (no cancer). I look at my
daughter and say, "Maybe he'll
come back to you, your child."

Weeping, we laugh.

7.

I receive your ashes, wrapped
in a blue velvet bag;
I hold you in my arms
like a baby, carry

you to my car, take
you home. Your ashes
aren't ashes, but white
ground crystals, specks

of darkness. Your bones,
your secrets (light
and dark) are safe with
me. I measure a cup,

dig you into your apple tree;
every year you turned the
soil in spring; now you
are the soil, bud, blossom.

The apple. Ripening. Into summer.
I place your crystals in my
bedroom. I dream of mountains,
eagles, the deadly, life-giving

Sun. I release your measured
crystals into a stream where egrets,
herons, wild ducks find sanctuary.
I weep to see the spray of light,

glowing, the dark, wet bank,
the softly flowing water
so close to the sea. High tide
greets all life here; how beautiful

your light, exposed to earth, creek,
sea, swirls of wind and rain (when
I return 2 days later, I laugh to find
a mess of beer bottles, an entire bottle

of Jim Beam whiskey, your favorite,
empty). Later, my daily morning rock,
the highest tides engulf it, today
not quite. Measured cup in hand, I climb

lower to meet the sea, spray wide,
showering sea, mostly stone. I feel
foolish, having missed the sea;
I sit and stare at my mistake;

anyone can see your crystals,
the light, the dark.
Shame, guilt, sorrow, that's me,
until the rising Sun strikes

stone, and I see your crystals
love the stone, they marry:
the sea explodes with life:
I see it: all life has come to bear

you home: the celebration.

8.

Once, when you were drinking,
you told me (at least 20 years
ago): "You always brought me
water in the desert."

You were born in the desert.
Your mother's name was Claire
(a piece of paper tells me).
You were born: Claire Lewis

McSpadden. Claire. Clara.
Clarity. A feminine light.
How well you hid it. But not
from me. This summer

I'll take a measure of your
crystals (a measure I'll keep)
to a sacred granite lake
in my mountains, where my eagles

know my voice and shadow,
my feminine light.
When I call,
when they come,

I will give this last measure
to the mountain, to the lake.
You loved these places as a young
man, and you always wanted to return,

I know. A dream: *You're young,*
in your Army uniform, you're so very
handsome, your spirit entirely intact,
you're standing on a field, smiling,

arms waving with excitement, waving
in your plane. "You always brought me
water in the desert."
These are the words

I'll say to the eagles,
to the lake, to the Sun.
Now I understand, father.
You always loved me

in that desert, Claire.

Reborn January 22, 1996

Fisherman in the Picture

I stand in the Salvation Army
staring at yellow daffodils,
laser art, as they call it,
leaping out at my eyes.

Your wife called, asking me
to pick something up for your
old room (where you left your
85 year old body behind),

something with yellow flowers,
she said. Your old room is
newly painted, a lamp where
a bare wire/bulb used to be;

a white, gleaming light switch
where a cracked one was; flowery
curtains, burgundy gauze in their
center, breathe in and out. You allowed

no one to repair or paint your smoke-filled,
cat-filled room. You enjoyed
the comfortable sleaze, stretched out
with your Kools, your cats beside you

on the bed, their cat food, water,
litter box by the dresser, and your
mouth delivering its usual dry wit
that always made me pause, laugh,

shake my head as though dealing with
a playful child, a terrible child
who sees no harm in speaking his own
version of prickly truth. So, I stand

staring at this laser art, thinking
of her request for something with
yellow flowers (for the new
walls); there's a laser lake, rippling

beside a laser stone path that leads to
a laser cottage; in the changing
light, it's eerie. I see you walking
up the laser stone path to the laser cottage;

and then I see you fishing on the laser
lake (you were a stubborn fisherman).
I even see you planting the yellow
laser daffodils (you were also a stubborn

gardener). I smile and almost walk
away, except for this seemingly dead
grey/black laser tree dominating the
foreground. It's sad and promising.

It speaks of endings/beginnings.
It's not pretty, almost frightening as
it shifts realities (death/life).
I don't see you planting this tree;

but I see you witness its cycles
(death/life/death/life). I buy
it for the beautiful, scary tree,
and as I hang it up on the new white

wall (she loves the yellow laser daffodils),
I hear you, "Jesus Christ, do I have to
look at this every goddamn day for
the rest of my life?

Couldn't you find anything
uglier?" I hear you laugh.
I see you on the laser lake,
pulling out laser trout for dinner;

large, dark, rainbow-scaled
trout. I see you frying them
up in the laser cottage, staring
out the window to the daffodils,

briefly, but mostly
to the life and
death tree,
father.

June 1996, 4 months after.

Voice

I dreamt Wolf Woman
singing in her tent,

next to me, singing
from her tent flap,

waking me up,
irritating me;

then I heard Bear
walking in her sleep,

moving by my tent,
so carefully, not

to disturb me,
to let me sleep

all night; and I
would have slept

all night, never waking
up if it hadn't

been for the Wolf
Woman singing with

all her longing, toward
the liquid stars,

so close; Bear
thinks she's walking

on the Milky Way,
that she will eat

all the food we've
hidden away from

her. Bear loves the
woman singing to the

light; she begins
to dance the ancient

dance of the Milky
Way. To the human

voice.

I wonder:
Do the others hear

Wolf Woman singing
from her tent flap?

Do they hear her
longing rising to the

liquid stars of
Milky Way?

Do they see Bear
dancing in their dreams?

Do they know Bear
loves the sound of

the human voice?
Singing. To the

Milky Way.
I wonder.

∽ ∾

Without Wolf Woman
and Bear we are

lonely in this
Universe. We

forget the dance
of the Milky Way.

We hide our food
from Bear

and we are
lonely.

∽ ∾

Tonight: Listen
to Wolf Woman

singing (even if
she wakes you

up): Tonight:
Listen to Bear as

she hunts your
dreams so quietly.

She is hungry for
your voice. Tonight.

> *Tuolumne, Yosemite*
> *(Uzumati: grizzly bear),*
> *June 1996*

Instructions in August

Behind me the Earth
cliff wall weeps,
and where it weeps
small, yellow flowers

thrive, centuries of moss,
thick, thick, thick
and soft, so soft,
comforts the Earth

cliff wall, as the
softness comforts me,
I touch it, know
I'm blessed because

this place, facing
the ancient sea, Her Tears,
Her Womb, that gave birth
to us, to me,

as I gave birth,
my tears, my womb,
and I wonder, Am I
soft enough, am I

strong enough
to comfort the world
as the Earth cliff
wall has done for

centuries. Earth's soft
tears strike stone: "You
must love someone more
than yourself, love life

more than yourself, love
the world more than your
self, love the Cosmos
more than your (self),

to give birth
to the Timeless One
who weeps forever into
the sun for joy,

my small, yellow flowers,
the magic that brought
you here, the Child
alive in the dying

body, love her,
love her more
than this life.
Weep into the sun."

August 1996, Santa Cruz

Letter To My Son

(on his 30th birth day)

We spoke early this morning,
our real talks we've had since
you were able to talk. 27 years
ago we talked about the things

that mattered to you: the best
bikes in your pre-school, more
apple juice, the kids you liked
and didn't like (grown-ups, the

same). The way you marched
right into groups of geese,
taller than you, yelling at them
to share your bread. Every mother

secretly (if she has the power)
raises her son to be the man
who might be capable of loving
her, and other women. In this

time, in this patriarchal time of
darkness, when the candle, the tiny
candle of the feminine soul must be
shielded by the beautiful and true

spirit of masculinity, I turn to you
(and other men like you), and say again –
Be a man of courage, of tender love.
Guard your (feminine) soul.

Is the soul feminine?
Is the soul masculine?
All I know is that she/he is
a small, sturdy child.

I still see you marching into the giant geese,
telling them to share.
Treasure that, guard that —
that fearless, loving child.

To Marc Jason, September 1996

The Crux

1.

Girl-child and amazon,
who I raised in the image
of She-who-I couldn't-name,
but dreamt and knew when

your body slid out of mine:
daughter. Loving you, I loved
myself — badly, exquisitely.
We clung, we fought, we separated;

you to the world of men,
and I in exile. I journeyed
to the Earth and back, seeking
you in the iris, stone, the seemingly

dead bulb; and, finally, I
had to let you go, forget you,
the features of my daughter,
until my own features became

clear, distinct: separate.
Myself. Woman. And I will
die alone, and so will you.
The rose never tires of blooming.

2.

She-who-I couldn't-name
comes to me in dreams
as I walk with dark-skinned
women. She is huge and

and I can't take her all in;
a belt of rainbow snakes encircle
her waist, gift of sun and storm.
Between us, daughter, lies a virgin land

where sun and moon rule,
equally; and in our loving
the land appears, vividly —
its mountains, deserts, orchards,

and the waves of natural boundaries.
Now I love myself badly — exquisitely.
Now I name the unnamable.
Now, I am your mother.

We will live and die separately,
each one virgin in her soul. The crux
of loving unsolved, but lived. The dream.
This wild rose belongs to no one.

But I offer it to you, anyway.

To Antoinette, at 39

Remembering Samsara

Lean into the sharp points.
   – Chogyam Trungpa Rinpoche*

I remember the light on my pale fingers.
I remember the dark on my thin eyelids.
I remember the pleasure of warm womb waters.
I remember the pain of being born born born.

I remember sunlight through the green leaves.
I remember smooth soft dust under my baby feet.
I remember cool water washing over me and over me.
I remember reaching for a Star, so far away in

the endless black sky, one night I looked, one Star
whispered, "Touch" – so my baby hands reached
beyond the crib, the open window
letting in cooling breezes from

the hot summer day, and I tumbled out
of my baby body, rushing to the Star,
that far away light that spoke:
"Touch."

And the Star gave me everything:
youth and beauty, strength and clarity,
humor and laughter, and so much joy
I opened my mouth and sang.

I was also given so much hunger (food, love,
love and more light). I was also given pain

* from *When Things Fall Apart* by Pema Chodron

which made me angry, and never ever broke
my spirit. I was given so much sorrow

which made me weep hard, sometimes with
shame; but what I found was this: at the
bottom of my sorrow, the very
bottom of my sorrow, and at

the farthest reaches, the very
farthest reaches of my
joy, is my Star.
But first I must tumble

out of my 52 year old body
(which is young and old,
strong and weak, beautiful
and ugly, utterly ecstatic

and utterly sad, utterly alive
and utterly dying, so new and
so used, female and male, in
pleasure and in pain, singing

and weeping and singing I am).
Tumble out of the comfort of bed,
the comfort of body, through
the open window (always

the open window), through
chaos   and   clarity,
I must die.
Again.

To touch my Star.
And then I remember samsara, lovely
samsara, awful samsara, wondrous
samsara, horrendous samsara, exquisite

samsara. I remember everything.
And I am grateful for each kiss,
each wound my body has received.
I gather them all (millions of

kisses, millions of wounds)
into a bouquet of
roses, such perfect roses,
dripping blood and the ripest

fragrance. This is my funeral
and this is my wedding.
These are the roses of samsara.
I am leaning into the sharp

points of their terrible
thorns (and I bleed),
to remember their soul's
ripe and dying fragrance.

Newly Born

Last night I dreamt
my newly dead aunt —

she was dressed in white,
so was I. She was

hesitant and shy until
I handed her a baby.

Then, she smiled at
the newly born.

December 1994

SACRED JOURNEY

Grandmother of Fire (The 13th Mother)

*"She has, in bonding to her infant, bonded to her heart
and has come into her own power, unlocking the insights on
which our species has depended for millennia. She has become the
mother, not just of that child, but of our kind.
And we do poorly indeed without her."*

— Joseph Chilton Pearce*

Japanese women walk into
the wind — one holding
a baby in her arms,
the other holding a baby

in her womb, about
7 months or so.
Pelicans in the sky
soar in groups,

graceful, gliding dinosaur
creatures (my cells
   remember them
   the silence their wings

created over my head
centuries ago, yes,
centuries ago — I was
a young mother destined

*From *Evolution's End*. (Also, read *The 13 Original Clan Mothers* by
Jamie Sams.)

to be dead, leave my
   body, late 20s
   or so, but it was
   good, life was good,

   my cells tell me;
   I am the ancestor
of my self and millions,
yes, millions — my family

of strangers, we birth
our selves century after
century, yet the Soul
is uniquely ours,

untouched, innocent,
   pure, as the
   silence of pelican
wings as they soar,

   as they glide over
our ancient heads).
Do you remember me?
I was the one who

loved the fire, the
miracle of the spark,
the warmth. I was
the one who wept

when the fire died,
and I was the one who
learned to hoard an
ember, one stubborn ember,

from the heart of
fire, keeping it till
dawn, wrapped in young
green leaves; and

then, the first time,
when it caught the thin
dry twigs, how we
laughed and sang,

laughed and sang,
as though we'd created
the Universe from an ember.
I was the young pregnant

woman, holding a year
old child in my arms,
and I was the ancestor
who learned the secret

of fire. How we
laughed and sang,
yes, how we laughed
and sang and cried for

joy. I am the
Grandmother of Fire, and
you've sat in this circle
for centuries, for centuries,

telling the same infinite
stories of victory and
defeat, birth and death,
fire and ice; the fire

in the sky that nearly
killed us all, but
didn't. I am the one
who remembers, who remembers.

I am the one who wept
when fire died, and
laughed when fire was
reborn.

I am the Grandmother
of Fire. Do you
remember me?
Do you remember me?

I am the 13th Mother,
Grandmother of Transformation,
and I remember you,
yes, I remember you.

I wrap your
Soul
in young green leaves
for ever.

Ancestral

To Jules, Jesus y Isidra
(my son, his great-grandmother
and great-great-grandmother)

Driving my son to high school
this morning, I see an Indian

from the corner of my left eye —
an Indian from Mexico, a campesino

with his straw hat and tassel
grazing his neck. His eyes are soft

but determined, he steps lightly
like a deer, he feels like prey

in the Land of Gringos; he hasn't
learned the rules, our ways.

My son doesn't see him until he's in
the back of the pickup truck, being

taken for his day of hard
work, cheap labor. "There's one

of our illegals," I tell my son
(great-grandson of a woman whose

eyes were soft but determined),
"going off to work very hard for

very little money. These people
definitely don't come here to sit

on their asses, they work fucking
hard." In a split second, I glance

at my 14-year-old son as he
looks into the eyes of the

campesino in the back of the
pickup truck, and my son's

eyes are soft. So
soft, but determined.

Santa Cruz, California

Hunting Transformation (The Grace)

The weather: hot sun, clouds gather,
hot sun, dark clouds gather, lightning,
lightning, blinding rain, tornado alert
in Denver, hot sun.

1.

Boulder. The mountains. The Flat
Irons. The 13,000 foot peaks.

Circling in. Landing. My 29 year old
son waits, perfect as the day

he was born. Later,
his cat brings in a live

green snake. I understand.
Transformation has begun.

"This cat's a hunter," Marc says,
laughing. "What a good cat," I say,

praising him, rubbing him
behind his delicate ears.

Marc lets the snake go. I tell
the cat, "And so am I," as he

purrs in my arms, then leaps, walks
away, tail high. Guiltless.

The innocent hunter of
transformation.

2.

I teach in a tent. These students
are willing to die here for at least

two hours. Transformation, we dare.
Transformation, we know, feel, laugh,

weep, write, say out loud in stories
and in poetry, oh transformation.

I become their teacher.
They become my students.

I become their student.
They become my teachers.

We are, all of us, warriors,
witnesses, magicians of this

alchemy we create. My gorgeous
lover, Death, sits next to me,

enters me, gazes out of my human
eyes; how he loves the human;

how he loves the hunt;
how he loves the taste

of living; how I love the taste
of transformation. When we make love,

only then, am I
fearless.

3.

Everything was worth this final class, their
final reading: the young woman to be

married in five days, demure at first,
in love, writes a poem about a Chinese

Amazon warrior, One Thousand Blades, her name.
Her husband, her children, killed in her presence.

She slashed through the enemy, sword in
each hand: One Thousand Blades, reads in

a full, strong voice, marries herself
in our wondrous presence, the grace.

Hurricanes in her hair, a lover's body;
her first poems, laments of lost loves,

lost men, betrayals (we all knew those
songs); her final poem captures "God's

Mind": "I am dying/and the world dies
with me/and is born/again, each time."

A dead childhood playmate, this woman
goes back to greet her, mourn her, transform

her, the old pain, the old fear.
This woman's eyes are calm: her poem:

a white snowy owl perched at the
foot of her bed and what that

meant all those years.
Another, with dark, dark eyes of an elk,

a poem to an elk accidentally killed,
then eaten: the gift, always

the gift of transformation.
The White Wolf Woman (wild

   blonde hair in a halo, eyes focused
to see) writes poems that break my heart,

then mends it: "I am me/made of love/
alpha and omega/the beginning and the end."

Poems of lovemaking. Poems of rage.
Poems of suicide. Poems of clarity.

Poems of transformation. Everything was worth
this final class. This, our wondrous

presence. This, the
grace.

4.

Later, at my own reading, I declare
like a fool: I LOVE YOU!

At the airport, a man brushes by
me, knocking my arm, hard, just

to stand in front, to be first;
like a fool, I stumble into him,

hoping to break his foot.
Now, I sit here (in Santa Cruz)

speaking to a pink/red/violet ROSE,
so sensual I want to eat it: I love you,

I murmur — each tasty petal, your secret
center given to bees, your black thorns

that draw blood without apology,
the roots I cut you from,

so selfishly, to witness your
final death as this rose. Your

scent in my memory; your scent in the
bud not yet formed, in the utter

darkness of soil, roots harsh with
the songs of live, green snakes.

> *To the Duende who did appear —*
> *Naropa, July 1996*
> *Boulder, Colorado*

Messenger From the Stars

To the great poet,
Messenger From The Stars,
when I met you at
a barbeque, I walked

right up and spoke
my heart; your eyes
shone, playful lights,
your 7 year old

grabbed me by the
hand, took me off
to a corner of the lovely
garden, Bobbie's garden,

and all her graceful flowers,
grown from tenderness and
love. And we talked.
You asked me if I'd

read KADDISH (the
   tribute to your mother
filled with rage, love, rage
   love; you saw

my mother's eyes
   and challenged me,
poet to poet).
I told you about my

father's death, how I
helped him die, and
that KADDISH was a work
of great love, great poet.

Your eyes (flash of
   lightning) filled
with tears and anger;
you remembered the time,

your reading. You kissed
my hand goodbye, and I
kissed yours. We met,
we played, we clashed,

we played. I'll see
you among the stars,
your light undying
   (You were a poet who

never stooped, who sang
   his soul in the body
of a 70 year old).
I see you among the stars,

your light undying,
enduring; in a
7 year old's eyes
you play.

To the warrior poet, Allen Ginsberg
(1926-1997)

                    In Bobbie Louise Hawkin's garden,
                    Boulder, Colorado July 1996

Ritual

"hoooooooo   aaaaaaaaah
hoooooooo   aaaaaaaaah
   aaaaaaaeeeeeoooooooh
   aaaaaaaeeeeeoooooooh. . . . "

I woke up chanting
this at 4 a.m..
I remember the ritual
of the deer, the song

to its spirit as it travels
far away to the moon,
to the stars, and
finally, to the Sun.

Driving with my son
and his friend (two
   young men) in the
night, a young antlered

buck leapt, smashed
himself to death,
hard steel, fast steel,
shut window, face

to face, the new
antlers graze my dreams.
I woke up chanting, "I love
you, if only I could've

killed you quickly,
skinned you, nourished
myself with your flesh,
honored your antlers,

made a fire, chanted
to your spirit as
it struggled free,
I love you, hoooooo aaaaaah"

This morning, one day
later, still dark,
Venus and a waxing Crescent
cling to the darkness

as the Sun reddens
life, bleeding light,
sharp shadows. O young deer, if
you must be sacrificed in this

unexpected ritual (the young men
    in my care), the Sun understands
this, the Sun understands this
            aaaaeeeeoooooh

To Jules and Damien
Santa Cruz — October, 1996

(A young deer, a buck, is always sacrificed to the
young hunters on their first hunt — we were unable to
honor your spirit within city limits — aaaaeeeeoooooh)

The Meaning of Life

On my way to my morning
walk, I see a young
man sitting on a fence
facing the sea, the

rising sun; below him
is a cliff; below that
death. He balances on the
edge, teetering slightly back

and forth. His face,
pain. I stop and watch
him (should I speak to
him, should I help).

The other day my 15 year old
son said, "Why are people
always talking about the
meaning of life, like who

really wants to know the
meaning of life, I don't."
I told him a story as
I drive him to high school:

"There's an old Zen story.
This young monk goes out to the
world searching for the Great
Diamond, you know, the meaning

of life, transcendence, things like
that. He searches until he's sick and
tired of searching, and by now he's in
his fifties. So, he returns to his very

ancient teacher, right? . . . who points
to his forehead, meaning the Great
Diamond had been there all the time
he was running around the world searching

for it." My son looked at me and smiled
(one of those stories): "Yeah, well, it's
like if I want to go surfing, I get my
gear on and get in the water." His voice

softens. "The other morning, just when the
sun was rising, a fog bank, and like it was
dark, was just sitting over our heads, like it
could crush us. Reminds you how little

you are out there."
"If everyone could remember that, we
wouldn't be in so much trouble globally,
you know?" "I guess."

Dreaming Zeros

I sit at the center
gathering rage,
sorrow, tenderness
DREAMS

for the present and
the future —
I was your soul
mate, but you refused

my soul, to die into
me, to give me your
darkness, and your
light. I, the circus

pony, the one with
one more trick up
her sleeve — I, the
magician, kept dying

into you, kept giving
you my darkness, and
my light. $1 + 0 = 1$.
$1 + 1 = 2$.

Are you the lonely
Zero Chief? Do you
know what that requires?
Zero is powerful, a self

contained circle, dying
continually into the
COSMOS — you must
love some thing more

than your self (or
     the Zero becomes
simply a number before 1).
I see your Zero Mask.

I see you hiding within
your circle. I see
your soul at the bottom
of the lake, singing,

waiting to be caught.
He comes to me in dreams,
is tender, he weeps,
makes love to me.

I see that you love
me, but a powerful
and lonely Zero Chief
refuses to die.

I sit at the center
gathering rage,
sorrow, tenderness
DREAMS

         ⌾ ⌾

In this web I die
daily, nightly. I know

how much I've loved
you, and what it is to

call back my soul,
my Zero that housed
her self in your soul —
she died for you, as I

would've died for you
with joy, with joy.
Now I know my
error in mathematics:

$0 + 0 = 0$. The COSMOS
Her Him Self. That's
what I wanted from you.
To die for joy.

To the Morning Star

Dreaming the Heart Open

I dream I find
your hand, take
your arm, wrap
it around me.

I tell you "I love
you" in that place
of waking dream —
you say it "I love

you, I'm so sorry,
I'm so sorry."
I don't want apologies,
just your arm wrapped

around me,
your hand
in my
hand.

                    To W.

              ∽ ∾

This dream opened my heart
wide open — I sent
you a poem and wrote
at the bottom "I dreamt

your hand" – There was
a time when you'd know
my message, when your
heart would open, once.

∞ ∞

At the beach I begin
to write – "Do you want to take
a swim?" I look up
to a wide open face –

"Do you want to take a
swim?" He's beautiful.
I'm frozen to the sand.
"Look, there's a baby seal

at the end of the beach,"
he points (a string barely
   rides his hips) –
finally, I see it, struggling

to survive – the beautiful
young man has called the
Mammal Rescue, and I'm
(secretly) thinking "I'm a

mammal, rescue me."
As we talk, I see his heart
in his eyes, wide open –
yes, his body is beautiful,

but his heart, his heart
is wide open, and I wonder

why men stop this, count this
as weakness to be outgrown —

leaving their wives, their
lovers, beggars of simple
tenderness, a glimpse
of wonder in shielded

eyes. This man could
be my son, but he's not
my son — he's a man
with wonder in his eyes,

confidence in his voice,
love in his heart for the
baby seal trying to survive,
curiosity about the cautious

woman on the beach with
pen and paper — he too
is a writer — as he talks
white light pours from

his face, his body,
and I see (so clearly)
I could love him, and
I do love him (for those

   moments) — my heart is
wide open, wide open.
I love his innocence
he gives to me.

                    ∞ ∞

This innocence has rescued
me — my innocence has rescued
me — yes, there's death, but
only of the body.

Yes, there's sorrow, but
only of the heart —
and pain, but only of
the mammal mind.

Then, there's JOY that
begins again, struggling to
survive — "Do you want to
take a swim?" Innocence.

To M.

Grief

> *"Dance, when you're broken open.*
> *Dance, if you've torn the bandage off.*
> *Dance in the middle of the fighting.*
> *Dance in your blood.*
> *Dance, when you're perfectly free."*
>
> — Rumi

The day is covered in tears.
My life is covered in tears.
The clouds are deep with darkness, moving.
My life is deep with grief, unmoving.

Sitting.
Setting.
Gouging.
Grief.

My grief feels like dying.
I am hemorrhaging from grief.
I am drowning in my own blood.
I am angry at my own heart, each beat.

I am angry because I've loved
too long, too well —
I am angry because Death takes the living,
and Time takes all children (their wonder,

    their innocence, if they forget the songs of
    their childhood — their secret songs

sung in the willow tree, the redwood tree,
under full moons as the fox paused to listen).

∞ ∞

If I could only find that fox, I would
feed her sweet chicken, fresh water —
I would ask her to sing me all the songs of
the living, all the songs of childhood she knows —

I would sit for days, weeks, years, until I heard them
all, every song she's ever heard —
and then, maybe, just maybe, my mourning, my grief,
would command me: STAND.

And maybe, just maybe, I'd stand.
And Grief would sing: "Did you think
you'd never meet me this way, so nakedly —
did you think this marriage would not take

place — did you think Joy would always keep
me bearable — didn't you know I am the lover
who prepares you for the sharpest, searing joys —
didn't you know I am the groom of Joy, this dance?"

∞ ∞

The day is covered in tears.
My life is covered in tears.
I follow clouds, raining over the ocean,
each wave, particle of water, weeps

and weeps, so beautifully.
I cannot weep all of my grief, but I
can walk, so I walk with billowing winds,
storming winds, leaning into wind and rain, I walk.

I follow the curve of cliff, ocean, grove of
eucalyptus — when I arrive, wet with grief
and strange wonder, I see it. A gift.
From the fox: leaves, sprouting acorns, weeds

and grasses, pieces of bright orange peel, shelled nuts, bark:
with her delicate paws, each piece, each object, became
a pattern of wholeness, a pattern of perfection,
on this worn, wooden table facing the creek,

flowing to the moving, dancing, tidal sea.
I witness the perfection of this gift, as the
wind creates new patterns here, new ones
there. I hear the fox laugh, as I weep with

strange joy and wonder.

Now, I see, I am the pattern —
whole, perfect, changing as
the wind sees fit.
I am the bride of Grief,

unbearable Grief, and my name is
Joy (that I exist). We will
dance in my blood and tears.
The fox is singing.

Fish and Wonder

My father's ashes in
Buck's Lake, a quarter
cup full, spread like
light, crystals of bone,

blood, temporary flesh,
spread like light on
the dark, soft earth
beneath the lake's windy

surface. Fishermen and fisherwomen
out in their boats, with children who
believe in fish and wonder; my father's
sun-in-the-sky blue eyes, how he

laughed at me when I borrowed his
fishing tackle, in San Francisco, to go
fishing from the piers. I brought back,
every time, enough for a meal, and he'd

fry 'em up dipped in buttermilk batter;
he'd say things like, "Girls don't like fishin',
much less guttin' a fish, but it sure don't bother
you none, in fact I bet you enjoy it," and he'd laugh.

And I'd act like I didn't hear the compliment
in his voice, see it in his eyes, and I'd say,
"I like to see what's in their stomachs, one time
I found a marble, a key, stuff like that." "Well, if

you ever find a diamond don't forget who lends
you the tackle, split it down the middle,
you and me," and he'd laugh. "If I ever found
a diamond I wouldn't tell no one," I'd say deadly

serious, making him laugh harder. "Keep yer
damn diamond, just bring back the damned fish!"
As I journey down the mountain away from
Buck's Lake, 7,000 feet into the sky (clouds

   and lake marry the sun; stars
and lake marry the moon).
Winding, winding, winding down,
I come to a small lake and stop

before the first crush of towns and
cities. Spread before me: lotus so
thick a bird walks across them, eating
bugs from their petals. Each lotus

bloomed wide in the noon sun; white,
sturdy petals with huge, round, green
leaves; yellow centers, pulsing.
I sit at the edge, in the shade,

and gaze, and gaze.
"I found the diamond, father,
and I know you saw it inside of
me. Now, I believe

in fish and wonder,
the temporary body's crystals,

memories, love, laughter, real sorrow,
the diamond. I treasure."

Sierra Madre, August 1997
(Vision at Gold Lake, my truth)

In the Fire

My sixteen-year-old son wrote,
"We all burn in the fire
called time," in an
essay for English —

a friend of his has
died — a sixteen-year-old
boy who never grew
larger than a four-year-old,

confined to a wheel-chair,
stubby legs that never
held him up as he ran,
jumped or simply walked —

hands that looked more
at home in the sea,
finlike and soft —
a large head for his

body, and he was black —
when he looked at you he didn't
mess around, he looked for
truth, and this was my son's

friend — my son, perfect
of limb, eye, foot and
hand, taller than me,
he runs steady as

an autumn wind,
blowing every ripe
leaf free —
he runs smoothly,

sweetly, as spring
and summer winds
coax the spiraling
leaf, then give

cooling, loving shade —
and I wonder, truly
wonder, how he
learned to love

so young, so well —
I remember going to
pick him up at his friend's,
finding them on the couch,

his friend in his arms,
like a baby, watching
cartoons — as they both
turned to smile at me,

simultaneously, I saw
two old men,
two old Buddhas,
who had found the

secret of life: love
and friendship. They were
ten years old. My son's
friend will grow up,

grow tall, become a fully
grown man, have lovers,
children — suffer, know bliss.
In the fire of my son's

heart.

To Bobby Easley (November 1997)

Shared Memory

"Where do I put him?"
you ask about your father,
a man who receded like
the horizon from your
memory — yet like the

horizon, it's always there,
just different, a different
part of the circle.
Then, I think memory is

more like a spiral of
circles — circles closing,
then spiraling on to their
endless journey. When I

think of knowing you,
I journey through many
spirals (from my womb
to the present you

who I love, admire
and respect). I say
this about your father —
you are his horizon

(whether he knows this
or not) — he journeys
toward you night and
day, never arriving to

his own peace, his own
fatherhood, the shared
memory of many spirals,
of loving you, now.

So, I say to you —
put your father in
your longing, in
the father you are

to yourself —
and the father
you are to
others.

> *To my son, Marc*
> *who has the courage*
> *to arrive, daily.*
> *November 1997*

License

Sun just rising, perfect.
Perfect stars melting into sun.
Perfect moon melting into Earth.
Perfect clouds in the sky.
Perfect chill on my arms. Face.
Perfect sea always dancing.
Perfect birds finding their nests.
Perfect music fills my ears.

This day is perfect, and I'm
here to say I praise my life,
my starring role in my own story,
my bit part in the stories of others.

Each time I returned to my unfamiliar
new body, did I have the wisdom
to say I love this life. . . .

Each time I returned with wide
innocent eyes, was I prepared
to say I love this life. . . .

This morning a total stranger paused
to say, "Do you have a license
to wear those shoes?" And he smiled
like the rising sun. And I laughed

that he saw the perfection of the day,
the sun, my bright purple tennis shoes.
I laughed because he gave me the license
of his joy. Perfect.

Sacred Journey

I visit the monarchs, clustered, floating
in the trees, in the sun —

then the Gateway Rock
to the sea —

the journey, always
the journey —

the wind scattered rose
petals on the grass —

I don't say my rose
or my grass —

I simply say rose,
grass — nothing belongs

to me — not children,
lover, father, mother,

or this body — only
this sacred journey.

I wear a crow's wing,
beaded from darkness,

rainbows within
the darkness,

rainbows within
the night, dreaming

night. I place my dreams
within this beaded wing.

I dream magicians
(men and women)
those I will know —
those who wait, my

circle who dream
me home. I dream
eagles hunting over
a Peruvian lake —

my Spirit Husband sits next
to me — I tell him, "That's
the way I want to
make love," as I watch

their powerful beaks open,
close — their prey cannot
resist them. I dream
muscular, sweaty lions

leashed to my wrists —
they pull me beyond my
endurance — I set one
free, but not the other —

I'm told, "That one may
turn on you," and so
I tune myself, tune myself
to this lion's heart,

and he tunes himself
to mine. Finally, I dream
beautiful Butterfly Men
who simply love me —

and how I love them —
how I've waited to know
such men — men with the
strength and gentleness

of butterflies. What do
I want? I want
to follow. This sacred.
Endless

journey. Where
the lion (who
is not mine).
Waits.

I gather butterflies —
I gather eagles —
I gather lions —
I gather magicians —

I do not see the
path, but I feel
it — it glows in
the darkness, the

beautiful and tender
darkness — I'm not
afraid of this darkness —
it's the darkness of dreams —

it's the darkness of a crow's
wing, beaded with rainbows.
I love this darkness —
I love this glowing path.

Stars appear to guide
my way — they fill
the night sky,
burning.

They were meant to burn,
to give their light.
My feet love their light.
The leashed lion on my

right wrist needs no stars,
no light, no path.
His desire. Creates a path.
I follow. This lion.

But I have tamed him.
To my heart. (After 53 years.)
And I hear him. Singing.
"I am the sacred journey."

November Dreams, 1997
Santa Cruz, California

DEAR IXCHEL

Las Dos Almas

*"The moment one begins dreaming — awake, a world of
enticing, unexplored possibilities opens up...Where the
unexpected is expected. That's the time when woman's
definitive journey begins."*

— Zuleica, in *Being-in-Dreaming,* by Florinda Donner

The two Almas — we
sit next to each
other, holding hands,
so tenderly — we

comfort each other, know
each other so very
intimately — our hearts
are on fire — we

bleed, yet save our
own lives, each Alma —
we share our fire,
our blood — she holds

the flow of blood that
I may live — I hold
the flow of blood that
she may live — las dos Almas —

how calmly we sit,
hand in hand, gazing
out at the immensity
of this Universe, this

journey, our lives —
one Alma wakes —
one Alma dreams —
we dream awake,

together, holding hands,
sharing fire, blood, memories,
our dreaming journey —
she cannot live without

me — I cannot live without
her — this, I finally know —
all these years of searching
for The Other has brought

me home to her — I will
never (ever) lose her —
she will never (ever) lose
me — we were born together —

we will die together —
we will journey home
to the stars (she knows
    the way — she is

fearless) — once in my
mountains, four nights in
a row, we did this —
further, further, till *my strength*

was gone — she fastened
her eyes on the starry
spiral till it pulsed
with light, the greatest

love I've ever known —
the light, la luz,
pulled us home — my friend,
my soul, mi alma, my undying

other — Twin Dreamer — all
those years I searched,
your hand was always in
mine.

>   *"Las Dos Fridas" hangs over my bed —*
>   *To Frida Kahlo, gracias.*

Real Magic

I am proud that my people believe
in magic
in beauty
in altars
in ancestors

that still speak to us in Dreams —
before and after my readings, I'm
led to altars built from memory
and love — altars for mother, grandmother,
father, grandfather, children who starve,

daily, in our world, and ancient Goddesses
and Gods who still know our hearts.
These are altars of such beauty
I can only stand and stare
and wonder

at the eyes, the hands, the souls
that contain, gather, re member to
create such perfect magic. Children
make an altar to the magic of words,
poetry, stories — those written, those

yet to be written, entirely decorated
with their poetry, their stories, rainbow
colors, rainbow lights, rainbow spirits
and rainbow souls. On television they
advertise tacos with a Magical Dog who

speaks with a thick Mexican accent,
"I theenk I looove youuuu. . . . "
O, Magical Dog — speak in Spanish,
gobble their tacos, hump that lying
TV. — it's not magic, only a tool

of magic.
In Dreams the ancestors say,
"We are the People of The Dog,
the far star, our home, howls
for us, howls for us. . . . "

O, Magical Dog, you are strange proof
that they can't silence the ancestors
who speak in many tongues, many words —
all the TVs, radios, phones, faxes, WWWs
can't take their place on the altar of

real magic.

*To the invisible forces that
guide us as a people —
And to the visible forces:
candles, words, faces, so
many faces and hands.*

*After readings in Sacramento
and Stockton, Las Gallerias,
Dia de Los Muertos, 1998 —*

Controlled Folly

For Carlos Castañeda, July 1998

Did you somersault into
the inconceivable?
Did you sneak past
the Eagle, your awareness

intact? Did you balance
terror and wonder?
Did you dance to the
folly of your death?

Did you sing to
the Ally? Did you
enter the Great Silence?
Did the silence become

White Light and Thunder,
cracking open the Gateway?
Did you become the lightning
the Eagle ate for one

second or forever, ever?
Did you laugh one
last time at the
terrible wonder of

human folly –
our stupidity,
our spirit?
As I lay here by the sea

in shredded fog, pelicans
gliding in wonder, small yellow
flowers blooming from
stone — some idiot throws

a can of soda from the cliff
over my head, just missing
me — some bored idiot reminds
me — my time on Earth is

perilous. Precious.

Chasing Buddha (at the end of the rainbow)

In crowded Curry Village (Uzumati: Place of the
Bear, Uzumati, Yosemite) —
I say to myself, "Everyone I meet is
Buddha" — the serene, the stupid,

the kind, the rude, the smiling,
the scowling, the seventy year old,
the seven year old, the sober ones,
and the drunks at 3 a.m. chasing

The Bear by my cabin, screaming, laughing,
shouting in English, Swedish, German, and
a few other languages — the one word they
say together as a mob is, "The bear, the

bear" — then a loud growl, their screams,
their laughter — "The bear, the bear. . . . "
Oh, great furry Buddha, this morning
I leap out of sleep before dawn in

the hopes that the international mob will
be hung over (or maybe you've eaten a few) —
I will find hot coffee, a muffin, watch the
great Sun fill soaring stone with its

great light, inch by inch by inch — in silence —
and I do — silence — later, as I slowly walk
the dawn-light path, I see two well
placed mounds of furry Buddha Bear

shit, remnants of its meals still
clearly visible — Buddha's gift
of shit, perfect piles, so serene
I laugh.

          ☜ ☞

My Buddha fellow travelers who
sleep in my cabin: my son Jules (17),
my grandson Cody (14), my granddaughter
Ashley (16) — all teenagers with quick wits, sharp

tongues, so I laugh every minute or
so — I love the uncivilized truth of
teenagers, so I join them, now and
then, to simply laugh.

Jules and Cody square off in a fart
contest, when one washes his hair the
other says, "You smell just like a mango,
bear food, dude!" Ashley wears a

bra top (with dignity and grace) which
makes pot-bellied men old enough to be her
father, stop, stare — I glare at them till they
look away (their 16 year old daughters

in tow) — other women wear bra tops, but
my granddaughter's breasts are luxurious —
I refuse to make her feel "indecent" — and so
I walk beside her, celebrate her beauty with

dignity and grace. Yes, I know her father would make
her hide herself — "Young woman, almost 17, never,

ever, be ashamed of your Buddha
beauty," I say (silently).

⊂⊃ ⊂⊃

Early morning, Ashley and I hike —
steep incline all the way UP —
a Rainbow Trail — first trees,
stone, trees, then the creek,

thunderous, the falls, wet trail,
rainbows of every size arching,
dancing, arching over leaping water,
stone, trail — we climb further, steps of

stone, further UP to the Blessing Place
where we stand in silence, sprayed,
drenched, soaked, blessed by
rainbows — "Look! There's the end of the

rainbow!" Ashley yells. I turn and see
rainbow's end melting in to stone. "Quick,"
I say, "Stand there, make a wish. . . . "
First her, then me.

She doesn't tell me her wish —
I don't tell her mine —
I think how wise she is (I don't have
   to tell her this) — the proper way to

become the rainbow, to
make an honest wish, to
receive the Buddha blessing,
and we laugh

freely —
the end
of this
endless rainbow.

∞ ∞

(Next day)

Pre-dawn morning, alone,
facing the infinite granite,
facing infinity, hot coffee in hand,
muffin in mouth —

"May I always find a perfect pile of
bear shit and the perfect presence of
rainbows as what they are —
the unexpected: gifts, blessings —

alien, irritating, so beautiful
I cannot speak, so maddening
I dare not speak, so perfect
I simply laugh to laugh with

wonder," I say (silently) to infinity
filling, inch by inch by inch, with
Sun, source, womb of all rainbows,
beginning and end. I am the

witness.
To the mundane.
To the miracle.
The end of

the rainbow where everyone
you meet is Buddha in
disguise. Greet them with
smile or scowl. Laugh.

Let them go.
Wish them well.
Let them go.
Laugh.

"You cannot guess their destinies –
you can only witness this moment.
Chase. Become. The Buddha.
Growl. (and) Laugh."

Yosemite Valley, August 1998

Pollen

("If I can't dance, I will crawl." bumper sticker)

Okay, I'll admit it —
I'm a 53 year old
teenager in love with
the world, her mysteries,

her safely guarded secrets
I always want to know —
and when I dance I know
(that's all I know) —

when my mind becomes my
body — when my soul
becomes my spirit — when
my life becomes the music,

then I know why
I came to be born
this time — this body,
this music. This dance.

(I am a ripe, red plum.
I am a ripe, red plum.
I am a ripe, red plum
waiting to be eaten

in summer. My womb
has ripened. My womb
has ripened. My womb
has ripened. A ripe, red

plum. The mystery.
I carry. The mystery
will eat it — again and again,
it will ripen, not for any

man, but for my pleasure.
Guide me, Pleasure.
Wise One. My womb.
I dance. To know.)

My 17 year old son and I
pull at the wishbone —
I win, but say,
"I hereby give you

half — half for you and
half for me." We laugh
and dance to his loud
punk music (I can barely

tolerate, but I dance
anyway to the Spirit
of Dance). My teenager,
my last and final

teenager. Now, I must
become my own teenager —
fearless, furious, ridiculously
ALIVE Spirit Of Dance.

(I am a ripe, red plum.
The mystery has devoured me.
I grow slowly in the
Womb Of The Mystery,

yet I dance with joy.
I need no name to dance.
I need only joy.
Do not name me, Mother.

Do not name me, Father.
That I may dance.
That I may dance.
To know. This mystery.)

The sunflowers on the table
rained yellow yellow
pollen
on the faces of my ancestors:

Frida Kahlo, Federico Garcia Lorca.
Their faces on my books.
They stare at me.
Covered in yellow yellow

pollen.
Oh, my ancestors, speak:
Tell me you wisdom.
Tell me your truths.

"Okay, I'll admit it —
in spirit I'm a teenager
who loves to dance and eat
the reddest, ripest plums. . . . "

They say.
Taking turns.
Laughing in the yellow yellow
pollen.

> *To Irma Orantes*
> *(Sister dancer, one who is*
> *ridiculously ALIVE – my friend*
> *of 40 years) August 1998*

In Spirit

A young man leaps
from a car, another
young man pursues
him — one begins to

weep (I've never seen
   a 16 year old male weep
   in public) — "Leave me alone,
you've kicked my ass, leave

me alone!" I walk over,
stand between them, offer
to take the bleeding one
home in my car — embarrassed,

he declines but thanks me —
the other one tells me to mind
my own business — I tell
him this is my business —

before I walk away, I touch
each one on the shoulder,
lightly — "Take it easy,"
I say, "take it easy."

The next day as I walk toward
the gym lockers, a young man
smiles and says, "Hey, I worked
out for you, so you don't have

to do it today!" I laugh
and thank him, realizing
the truth — these gifts
are possible —

to give, to take —
they return
and return,
in spirit.

The Vest

She was my best thing. – Sethe*

I wear the vest you
gave me for my 49th
birth day – I wear
it to readings, and

tell the wonderful strangers,
my readers, "My daughter
gave me this vest – she
sewed all these charms

on it, isn't it beautiful. . . . "
And I think it – "She was
my best thing" – but I
don't say it, and the

women gather close to
see the magical charms
you spent hours choosing and
sewing onto this purple rainbow

vest (purple, my favorite
    color) – the women see
it right away, the silver
heart with a purple

ribbon sewn right over
the heart-place: "She

*from *Beloved* by Toni Morrison

gave you a purple heart!"
they exclaim, laughing —

then the Goddess, dancing
on a crystal — a skull, death's
wisdom opposite, held
by clear circles

the color of bone —
a fierce owl, held by turquoise
ribbon — a gentle rabbit, a singing
fox, a rainbow heart

that's never suffered,
that's only sung and
danced, known joy —
a golden frog, heaped

with jewels, and a chicken
that laid the golden
egg — the rest are
crystals, beads and beads,

strung purples, reds, greens,
topaz blue and blues, golden
yellows, just beauty, just beauty.
The women know what

I'm thinking ("She was my
     best thing") — one woman
takes off her earrings,
quotes an ancient poem,

"Daughter, you are more
precious than jade."

She hands them to me, strung
with turquoise and jade.

Her eyes fill with tears,
my eyes fill with tears —

she tells me silently —
"You are your own best

thing." And now I tell you,
daughter — "Treasure your own
daughter, yes, she is the
dazzling new one at 17 —

and know that the purple
heart you gave me is not
one of sorrow, but *JOY*. . . .
You are your *own,*

you are your very
own
best best
thing."

        ∽ ∾

For   give
For   get
Re   member
Your   Self

For   give
For   get
Re   member
My   Self

The	gift
We	give
The	gift
We	receive

Receive this.
Gift.
As I receive.
Yours.

Your rainbow
vest
that told me,
that sung me,

"You are your very
own
best best
thing, Mom."

∞ ∞

Re   member
how your perfect daughter, you
in a sexy sarong, and I
went dancing.

Re   member
how we took food and
champagne to the beach, then
swam, laughing.

Re   member
how we backpacked to

Gold Lake — lightning, thunder,
rainbows, laughing.

Re   member
how I treasured you,
how I treasure you,
"Daughter,

you are more precious
that jade." Tell this,
tell this to
your daughter (your son).

What I re   member
is your perfect laughter,
your perfect joy —
your child's heart

that never suffered —
that only sang,
that only danced.
That rainbow

heart. *(Where*
you are
your own
best best thing.)

To my daughter, Antoinette —
November 1998

Beyond Beauty

> *It was yours from the day you were born.*
> *You lost it, but I found it for you at the bottom*
> *of the sea.*
>   − An old fisherman*

You ask, what does
my treasure look like . . .
all my life, since my
earliest dreams

I dive
I dive
I dive
I dive

into the sea,
the beautiful womb sea −
creatures stalk me,
protect me, play with

me as I dive and
swim and dream −
all my life I've been
diving, I've been flying

to the bottom of the utter ly   beautiful
womb mystery source of life
SEA   OCEAN   LA   MAR
and you ask me what my

*from *Shabono*, by Florinda Donner

treasure looks like. . . .
Close your eyes,
dive with me,
fly with me,

dream with me . . .
in this ocean you may
breathe, the creatures
know you — in this ocean

mystery your wonder must
always equal your
terror, your wonder must
always equal your

terror . . . or you'll
drown, turn back,
say there is no
womb mystery source of life   OCEAN

LA   MAR . . . you'll say
there is no treasure,
your soul will cease
to sing and long for

the bottom of the womb
mystery source of life   OCEAN
LA MAR . . . now, close
your eyes (wonder and

terror singing in your
soul the perfect music
you heard at birth as
you swam into the light

from the bottom of the
wombmysterysourceoflife) —
yes, close your eyes,
dream with me . . .

now, open your hand
slowly   gently —
the treasure you were
born with, never lost,

never lost, only for
gotten, only for
gotten — memorize this
wonder, this terror, this

terrible beauty
that burns, that soothes
the palm of your hand,
your dreaming eyes that

open   open   open   open
re   member   re   member
your for gotten
treasure, it is yours

(your dreaming eyes are
open   open   open   open)
for ever and ever —
when you swim,

when you fly, fly
from your body one
time, one time, and never
ever re turn to

your body
this body
this time
this life —

when you fly, fly
from your body,
when you dive into
wombdark   sunlight,

you will sing your *perfect*
song, you will be
come terrorwonder —
you will be the treasure

you have held
you have *seen*
with your   open   open   dreaming
eyes —

now, friend, my left
hand opens slowly   gently —
this treasure, this gift,
this breath, this moment,

this treasure, this gift,
this breath, this moment,
this one time, one
time, beyond beauty.

(And I, my friend,
I have never, not
ever, begged for
mercy.

I see it in your   open
open   open   dreaming
eyes, I see it, the
mercy.)

Hunting Beauty in April

We arrive in a field of
softest blue forget-me-nots,
the poison oak, stinging
nettles, and new long

green grasses over the
dead — we arrive to see
white virgin blossoms on a
tree so old, this one's

conquered death for
our eyes to see
perfection — we arrive
as three stallions graze —

one white, one black,
one auburn — each one
so powerful, I bow
my head in wonder as

we greet the white one,
the auburn one — we try
to greet the black one,
but he snorts and paws,

moves away, muscles dancing
for our eyes to see —
this one, the black one,
is a gift from the Mystery —

this we cannot touch,
but we can see it with
our own two eyes —
we can pass it on,

these gifts of perfection,
arising from imperfection,
if only we can
see.

To Leon —
Pogonip, Santa Cruz, 1999

Wake Up

After my reading in a
Catholic church, daring
to say it's time for
the symbol of a crucified

divinity to be replaced by a healing
divinity (for the next 1,000 years) —
please, may we begin the healing
now now...and in San Diego to

rooms full of students and
teachers who came to face
the lightning with me,
the lightning in my words,

my poems, my life, our lives,
in this final year of our
century...
after my readings

I found myself on a 14 mile
dirt road, descending into the
Valley Of The Womb (Tassajara
Zen Center) — rocks in the

road force me to stop,
turn off my car's engine, brakes
on, leap, lift the rocks, heave
to the side of the road, over

and over and over —
dusty, sweaty, fearing to
break an axle, I mutter,
"Before enlightenment pile rocks,

after enlightenment pile rocks" —
but of course, this is just
my life (and everyone else's) —
what's piling rocks compared

to being force-marched,
breast feeding your baby,
your toddler lost in the
chaos, your husband shot

before your eyes, your
sister raped, your brother
beaten beyond recognition,
your parent's house torched,

you cannot hear their voices
even in dreams — there's
too much suffering,
too many crucifixions —

you can only dream silence,
blessed silence,
healing silence,
split by gun fire, bombs, screams, the endless weeping. . . .

When I reached the Valley of
the Womb, I entered
Her Healing Waters, facing
Venus through wise oaks,

until Venus set in darkness —
the other stars blazed
forth for ever and ever —
I was alone in Her Healing Waters,

yet I'm never really by my
self — we are here to wake
each other up, wake each
other up...outside the Zen Temple

a wooden gong says:
WAKE UP WAKE UP
DO NOT WASTE YOUR
LIFE   WAKE   UP

It's worn in the center,
mallet to gong —
the sound of wood,
the sound of the Universe

WAKE UP WAKE UP
DO NOT WASTE YOUR
LIFE   WAKE   UP
We are, each one of us, we are

the healers we've waited
for these past, dark,
crucified centuries
WAKE UP   WAKE UP

To César A. González-T.
(And to a young black man who
told me, after a reading, his African
name means, "God has returned.")
— May 1999

Her True Self

> *True rebels is not who you believe them to be or*
> *who you decides them to be, but who they is. And*
> *they true identity, they true self, is nonnegotiable.*

> — Mosquito*

I cut my hair —
why did I cut
my hair, my grown up
girlie hair (which I

   love, I'll admit it) —
why did I cut those thick
curling curls, whispering of
the Nile — why did I

cut the sweep of hair,
my curtain, my veil —
why oh why did
I cut that part of me

away — the sexy vixen,
something like that —
the sex object, the slave,
the closet pleaser —

the girl who had to grow
up to be a woman —
but there was joy and
pleasure, births and

*A character from the novel *Mosquito* by Gayl Jones

transformations −
I loved the woman,
I worshipped her,
but she hardly noticed

me, yet she needed
me (her true self)
to survive, thrive, deal
the killing blows,

and then the gentleness,
the tenderness I always
gave her, the healing
she couldn't live without −

me. The girl, the girl
who had to grow up
to be a woman −
I'm here with my short

sassy hair, laughing
and dancing around my
54 year old face of
girl/woman   woman/girl

and she will love me −
and she will love me
as I have loved her from
the beginning. I was her

sword and shield −
she was my Mistress −
now, there's just me
with short hair.

Before I looked into
someone else's eyes
to see if they might
love me, or if I even

existed. Before I was a
Mistress or a slave, and
I knew the true, harsh
freedom of a girl.

Before the world held up a
mirror and said LOOK,
my eyes could see the burning,
beautiful, awful truth that kept

trying to kill me, heal me.
The woman is my
true self, and I am —
I am surely hers.

The Sky

The door is round and open.
Don't go back to sleep.

– Rumi

When the children really
leave you (at 38, 36, 31),
and the 17-year-old
impatiently dries his wings –

when the 52-year-old husband
of 20 years moves in with
his 30-year-old ex-student,
feeling sorry only for himself –

when the 38 and 36-year-old
"children" become middle-aged
whiners, blaming you (not
their absent father, the first

husband) for their normal,
boring, neurotic tics – and
they don't quite understand,
they could've been born in the

middle of a massacre in Rwanda,
a bombing in Baghdad, or had
to fetch food and water down
Sniper's Alley in Bosnia –

no, they whine, "I'm not
a millionaire or famous

or love my life, my mind,
my heart, my body, and

it must be your
fault." I'm bored.
By the tics. The 31
year old holds my interest,

loving motorcycle rides in the mountains,
sun rise, sun set,
ribald and goofy humor,
and I'm sure sex.

The 17-year-old can't help
himself, this drying of
wings, this testing of
wings — surly, confident,

charming, humorous —
he doesn't whine —
I cheer him on —
"See that sky?

It's only life, so
wide and enticing.
Blame no one.
Thank every one.

For their part.
In your awakening.
How you woke up.
And love the sky."

Is this the sky of
my childhood?
Is this the sky of
my dreams?

Is this the sky I
breathe in at birth?
Is this the sky I
breathe out at death?

Is this the sky of
my laughter?
Is this the sky of
my tears?

Is this the sky of
my desire?
Is this the sky of
my innocence?

Is this the sky of
terror?
Is this the sky of
wonder?

I breathe the sky in,
freely.
I breathe the sky out,
freely.

There is a price to freedom
I have always paid.
The willingness, no matter
how painful, to

wake up.
Child's eyes.
Child's eyes.
I see.

The sky.

Dear Ixchel

Those who run are the life that
flow in our people.

– N. Scott Momaday*

Who is this son I remember
within my body?
Who is this son born at
7 months, who I wrote
prayers for, to heal his
    eyes, lungs, heart?
Who is this son that made
me face the lightning with him
    at 8 months old, to teach
    him, me, fearlessness?
Who is this son that rarely
cried and always laughed
    out loud just for joy,
    just for joy?
Who is this son that
charmed me?
Who is this son that
exhausted me?
Who is this son I taught
to bike ride, and swim
    in Mother Ocean?
Who is this son I gave
    to Mother Ocean?
    Mother Earth,

*from *House Made of Dawn*

Mother Cosmos,
Mother/Father Cosmos?
I could barely let him go.
I can still barely let him
go.

Was this the son I tip-toed
to kiss goodbye, Ixchel,
as he prepared to fly far
away to one of your
    floating Turtles?
Is this the son who pierced
his tongue in the
ancient way of Quetzalcoatl,
Feathered Serpent — Mayan God,
both male-female, light-dark,
Earth-Cosmos, God-Goddess . . .
is this the son? Is this
the son,
Ixchel?

This son is a runner, as
all my sons have been
runners, breath
and body straining,
feet drumming
Earth, her body,
their life streaming
forth (mystery to
mystery) — yes,

this son is a runner. . . .

Ixchel, take my son, let
the floating, singing
Turtles call him
son, this young
man in the arms of
the Earth, her passion.

     To the traveler, Jules
     New Zealand, July 1999

Release

I travel through my
past, I fly
through my past
until I reach the

room of my regrets
where things are lost
and tattered, tinged
with sorrow, longing,

grief, such longing
to heal to heal to heal –
a man, hidden in the
corner, leaps to hold

me, he is stronger than me,
but he's cautious of
my strength – he pours
liquid over me, and I

fear he's going to burn
me, then he laughs
softly, very softly –
this oil soothes me

as the others come to greet
me, softly laughing –
I hear them singing, now, in
this room of release.

Dream, April 1999

DEAR WORLD

February 18, 1998

Dear World,

The people of my planet, Earth,
don't realize they're in
PARADISE –
you see, all the false myths

told them – century after century –
they've been driven from,
they've been excommunicated from,
they were torn, lost, separated from

PARADISE
because they've *sinned.*
They ate ripe fruits, you see,
and they were the sweet, wise

heart of Earth speaking to them.
They drank pure waters, pure as
the souls they were born with,
and they heard the Earth, the Universe,

laugh with pure abandon.
And in their innocence they made
love, they made love in PARADISE,
and they desired nothing more than innocent

pleasures, and they worshipped PARADISE
because *they were in it,* and when they killed

it was for hunger, life, and they were
grateful.

What I wish for my people (and myself)
here on Earth, in the coming century,
the new millennium, is that we
begin.

We begin to let the false myths
fade. We begin to know the myths
of our planet, to eat her ripe, sweet
fruits, to hear her heart speaking.

We begin to know the taste of
purity and innocence — the waters
and desires of our Earth, our Universe.
Our birth right: innocence, laughter, tears, healing.

We begin to see, know, understand —
each child pushed forth from the
womb, seeking breath and
home is born without sin in

PARADISE.
We begin to kill (when we must) from
true hunger, true gratitude. We begin
to weep, also, for *the enemy,*

what we've become,
what they've become.
What we can be (in Paradise)
What they can be (in Paradise)

In January, a pregnant whale,
journeying south, paused here

to give birth in Paradise, always
in Paradise, dear World.

Monterey Bay, Santa Cruz

September 30, 1998

Dear World,

I am not afraid of winter —
I know her terribly beautiful face
of ice, snow, temporary death —
her serene smile in January,

her whispers, "Live   now   live   now" —
her sacred presence at the feast —
her sacred presence at the famine —
her sacred presence in my daily life

whether winter, spring, summer, fall —
she dreams me dead, unborn, born
NOW   NOW   NOW   NOW —
at 54 my face becomes more like hers,

her winter, spring, summer, fall —
I turn my face toward Kosovo where
over 50,000 people (children, women, men)
crouch in the forest, hiding from crazed men

who wish to kill them over borders that
exist only in their minds — she sees this,
and nods at the first snowflakes (their terrible
   beauty) — she closes her eyes as children

dream of warm food, warm beds — they play
in their dreams, they play in their dreams
as she closes her eyes. I face Kosovo
and plead for mercy.

October 8, 1998

Dear World,

I drove into my mountains with trust —
from my home by the sea in spring —
from the valley still hot in summer —
from the lotus blossomed lake in foothills —

into my mountains with trust —
then a mist of rain like baby tears blessed me —
then a WALL of rain blinded me, no vision —
then hail the size of large marbles, crashing

onto my windshield, the Sky a child at play —
and then snow, so soft, so soft,
the Goddess laughed and laughed, my fear
of ice, naked tires clutching road — so, I

slowed to watch the wonder, to honor
Winter, Death, Her Power to destroy, to create,
to dazzle me with blinding light — as the softness
of her laugh surrounded me, I knew

I would follow Her anywhere (even Death, that
    open, spiraling gate of souls, of birds who fly,
who fly to freedom). And so, I began to smile as
my tires skidded on the Child's marbles, Her

soft soft snow — She always knows
what I want for my birth day (in this

body, this time . . . October 4th). The gift
of the newborn's grace. To trust your wonder,

dear World.

> *(To Adelita, who waited with her garden full of*
> *rainbow flowers, ripe squash, pumpkins, chilled*
> *champagne —   con milagros en los ojos.)*

October 21, 1998

Dear World,

Ixchel sits with me
on my towel facing the
sea (this beautiful
   day, this perfect

day). She walked with
me – she swam with
me – and now she
spreads her butterfly

wings (yellow, purple,
   red, black) – she dries
them in the sun, the
warm Indian summer sun –

she is so beautiful
I weep with joy –
she smiles with perfect
sorrow – her wings

caress the warm October
air, rainbow wings, oh
her rainbow wings touch
my face so softly:

"Ixchel," I say, "why
is it easier for humans
to hate than love –
why is it easier to

cause pain than pleasure —
why is it easier to see
the ugly, and why is it
harder to see the beauty —

why is it easier to be
bored, jaded, in misery,
and why is it harder to know
wonder, innocence, ecstasy —

Ixchel, were you with him when
he screamed and suffered —
did you wrap your rainbow wings
all around him, all around him,

so gently, so softly, all around
him — did you lift
his pain — did you lift
his pain — did you heal

him with wonder, innocence,
the ecstasy of your smile —
did you give him peace —
did you open your fertile,

always fertile womb, Ixchel —
was there room for one
more — did the Ancient Child
you carry (who is so

   pure shehe is both
femalemale), did the
Ancient Child greet him —
and why is it easier for humans

to hate than love, and
did you wrap your
rainbow wings all
around, all around him?"

Slowly, with blinding beauty,
she lifts from my towel,
from the sand —
her pregnant belly ripples

with life, and I hear the
Ancient Child singing
in harmony, voices mingling
wonder, innocence, ecstasy —

voices so pure
they are femalemale.
Dear World,
I tell you this because

I know how hard it is
to remember harmony, and
then Ixchel came today (always
    pregnant with the Ancient Child, singing).

Then Ixchel came today
in perfect beauty (edged
    with horror), in perfect
love (edged with hate),

in perfect pleasure (edged
    with pain), in perfect
joy (edged with sorrow).
She enfolds us in her

vulnerable, indestructible, delicate, powerful,
human, inhuman rainbow wings.
She wraps her wings all around,
all around us, forever,

dear World.

> *To Matthew Shepard, a 21 year old gay man*
> *beaten to death in Laramie, Wyoming,*
> *October 1998 – and may we learn to love*
> *ourselves in the other.*

November 19, 1998

Dear World,

Wedged in the sand,
low tide, I pick it up,
a triangle of glass,
clear glass, sharp edged

glass — I wash it in
the tide, offer it to
the Sun — rainbows
dance through the triangle

of glass — I see
Honduras flooded,
their dead embraced by
mud and water, the great

body of Our Mother —
Nicaragua, Guatemala,
Mexico — Ixchel wanders,
gathering souls in her

Star Basket, covering
them with her
Sun Blanket, she takes
thousands home

to rest, re member
why they come,
why they choose to
re turn.

Each soul (el alma)
a spark (un chispa)
Ixchel gathers in her
Star Basket (paz y luz) —

she sings, "*Sparks of the
Sun, there is no death —
guests of the Womb, the Mystery,
there is only re turn and re turn —*

*re turn   re   turn
to the Sun,
to the Mystery,
re turn to the*

*STARS
I gather you in my
Star Basket, perfect essence,
la vida...."*

April 13, 1999

Dear World,
        Dear Ixchel,
                Dear Grandmother,

Grandmother, give me your
strength —
Grandmother,
give us your
strength —

Bombs fall   fall
Bombs fall   fall   fall   falling
bombs fall to stop the
KILLING

Within vacation time, hours
from Paris, Rome, London —
we see them instantly
on TV, the web —

Ixchel, Ixchel,
we hear their stories —
story after story after
story — they make us

weep — miles of people
walking — old women, old men,
small children, a young woman
breast feeding her baby

with her beautiful breast,
her eyes have seen
and seen and seen
death, un natural

death, cruel in human
cruel un natural death –
a young boy trying
to hide is killed

in front of all –
a young boy watches
his sister, each sweet
sister, his mother, his only,

his mother killed in front of
his own, his own two
young boy eyes, then
they shoot his young boy

body, torch his house,
this he sees, this he sees –
a 5 year old girl is lost
in the mountain snow –

can you imagine, can I imagine,
losing your my 5 year old daughter –
would I rather die, would
I, would you? Rape and

bland sys tem at ic horri fic
cruelty, can I, can you,
can we imagine....
grandmother and 15 year old

grandson are shown on TV —
soldiers were beating him,
dragging him to his
death — grandmother held

on, wouldn't let go,
grandmother held on,
wouldn't let go, wouldn't
let go — one of the soldiers
      (seeing *his* grandmother)

said "RUN!"
Grandmother Ixchel, give us
your strength as we
run

Give us your
strength
as we crawl walk
run

Give us your strength
as we crawl walk
run into the new
century....

Hold on to us —
don't let go —
hold onto us —
don't let go, Grandmother.

Ongoing genocide in Kosovo

April 25, 1999

Dear World,

Ixchel sent me this dream:
two young boys, twelve
or so, take me to the
place where young boys

dream together, so peaceful,
a flowing creek, like
birds we fly in —
as I look up, I see

fishing lines, countless
fishing lines streaming
from a bridge where
boy's bare feet dangle

and swing so peacefully —
this place where boys
dream together (if if if
    they can still reach

it, dreaming, dreaming),
I've seen with my own
three sons (three young
    boys), the years I

fought to keep them
safe, in peace, I
glimpsed it in their
play, their laughter,

their dancing eyelids as
they slept the sleep of
children — in my dream,
under the arching bridge,

hoop of rainbow pulses,
calling the boys to manhood —
they raise their arms, in
joy, to fly into the

pulse of rainbow, pulsing,
glowing, singing, "Be men
of good heart, be men
of good heart, swallow

the colors of the Sun,
our Sun, as you
leave your boyhood —
you are my sons

for ever and ever —
I hold you in my hands —
you hold me in your hearts —
be men, be men, be men

of good healing heart."
Ixchel, if young boys
lose their way to your
Dream of peace, safety,

do they forget your
Rainbow lodged in their
healing hearts, do they
kill the world, Ixchel?

> *Two boy/men kill in Colorado, April 20th, on Hitler's*
> *(once a dreaming boy) birthday*

SACRED ONE

Sacred Baby

They say the 13th Tree
in the circle,
in the center,
is weakest, therefore

is strongest,
is the one in the center
that's open to every voice,
every word, every song

not heard. This Tree
houses the 13th Nest
where the strange and new
begins, what's most needed

for the unknown future,
what hasn't even been
dreamt yet, still waiting to
be born in the 13th Nest.

What is weakest in me,
what I dread the most,
you my weakness, my
skinny fledgling bird, poking

through your shell — each
time, each time you've

taught me a brand new
song, given me brand new

eyes and brand new, brand
new wings — O my bird,
my weakling bird, I cannot
describe your wings or

the flight always mapped at
your birth — I can only
wonder at the power of your
eyes that call me.

⚮ ⚭

I was three years old, the three
adults...my grandmother,
mother, aunt, didn't
know what to do —

I remember some one was
coming to our house,
coming inside to harm them,
to harm us —

I remember their fear
as the door knocked,
a hand saying . . . let me
in, let me in. . . .

I remember a woman
coming in (the landlady
    my aunt told me) — I hit,
kicked, screamed, she left.

I, the weakest, the baby,
saved us — I was the
13th Tree and in my frail
branches, the 13th Nest was

built, twig by twig, with every
imaginable object gathered from
the world the 13th Nest was
built, until finally in my

29th year the strange,
beautiful, awful, weak and
sacred bird came to rest, came
to birth her young in my branches —

when the new horribly new,
when the new wonderfully new
song is born, I listen, add
the song to the world-wide

chorus of new born
songs. Trust the baby,
the weakest part of us,
that saves us —

trust the Queen (or King)
who cradles the baby,
the strongest part of us,
in her warrior arms.

*To Leslie Simon (who honors the baby
and the warrior) –
San Francisco, July 1999*

Sacred Child

First we joined voices,
spirits by your fountain —
we laughed and wept
for ourselves, for the

world as we usually
do — all around us the
mountain listened to the
songs of our voice —

next morning we packed
clothing, food, wine....
climbed the path to
our lake, greeted air,

the eagles with our shouts —
swam in numbing silk,
let our Sun bring us
life — that night two

young men carrying flash
lights in the moonless
night, talking and yelling,
found our lake — finally,

they slept on their side,
we slept on ours — in dreams

we probed their desires,
their gifts to the Goddess

and us — enjoy this
time, enjoy this
time of our, this
sacred ripening —

let out heart and mind,
let the Goddess and God,
let ourselves and others
ripen in

the utter
mystery
of our
sacred wombs.

May that
child
be called
Pleasure's Wisdom.

To Adelita S. Meyers
Las Sierra Madres, Plumas
July 1999

Sacred Teenager

We speak of waking, and
we speak of dreaming —

we speak of masculine, and
we speak of feminine —

we speak of The Critic, and
we speak of The Creator —

what I know is this:
we must be fully human:
love, give birth, suffer and
sing, know the history of

our species, claim it as
our own family story
unfolding: gaze at the
unspeakable cruelties, the tenderness,

never ever look away,
but witness without hope,
and from that hope our
sacred vision will come:

the first vision we should have
received at 15, the gateway
age, but perhaps were too
busy fighting with the world,

trying to survive our innocence.
Now, yes, now welcome the
Sacred Teenager who receives
and creates her sacred

vision — why she was
born — why she was
chosen to bring her raw, wild song to
this chaotic, perfect symphony.

To Carmen H. Nuzum
Dinner, talk at sunset, Santa Cruz —

Sacred Woman

I go to praise the Goddess
Tara with a friend —
we go to The Land of Medicine
Buddha — we are the

only people — the Buddhist
nun faces us, tells us
to place mother, father
beside us — friends behind

us, enemies in front —
I place Goddess to my left,
God to my right,
my friends and enemies

all around me — I have
no enemies except my
own ignorance (we meet,
we meet) — we chant

"Praise to Tara" nine times
(21 homages) — I'm tempted
to bolt, but She
appears. . . .

"Tara, swift, heroic!
Eyes like lightning instantaneous!
She whose face combines 100
autumn moons at fullest!

Blazing with light-rays
resplendent as a thousand
star collection!" (There are
21 verses times 9)....but I

see Her, I see Her....
I see She is
a woman....
I see

She is
a woman
as I am
a woman —

She has created...."Filling
with HUM, Desire, Direction, and
space! Able to draw forth
all beings!" Yes.

She has destroyed...."Putting
Her feet left out, right back,
blazing up in raging
fire-blaze!" Yes.

She is
a woman
as I am
a woman. Yes.

> *To Carmen León,*
> *Full Moon, July 1999*
> *(and to the Perfect One –*
> *Tara, Ixchel, La Virgen)*

Sacred Warrior

I race to the other side
of the beach toward
rocks still warm from
day at sun set —

I climb to the top, sit
and watch, then I see it,
Venus, bright star, why I
came — an older woman

walks her two dogs, leans
on a cane — I imagine her
two children, her husbands
gone, her children on the

other side of the continent
or the other side of the
world — she is in this world
at sun set, leaning

on her cane at dusk as
teenagers begin to appear
carrying wood, food, illegal
beer, laughing — I remember

my four teenagers, how
I let them go to life, and

I remember Venus, Sacred
Tara, Ixchel, as I watch her

walk with confidence into
darkness, Venus as our
witness — we are
warriors

of first blood,
of the cradle,
of last, wise blood,
of our worlds, the dusk,

and Venus. She
who loves
to love her world.
The power. To love.

To a stranger,
Early August, 1999

Sacred Queen

My garden is a mass of
dandelions (first bright
  yellow), some peach
roses (blooming, dying to

  secret seed), a lemon
tree (with no lemons), water
for birds and cats (hunter
  and prey take turns), a

small clay container for
fire (small spiders make
  it home) — and one,
solitary orchid that blooms

alone
long after the others,
months ago — she isn't
lonely in her stubborn

beauty as she faces
sun, moon, stars, shadows —
she is the Queen of my
garden, we dream together

day and night as
dandelions become

translucent
fertile wishes....

I am
created
as I
create.

(To my womb)

Sacred Sun

"She who is like the Sun" —
we find this Buddha
in Stanford's museum,
a thousand Buddhas

carved into her
base, a thousand
universes, the swastika,
ancient symbol of for

ever, etched in gold over
her heart, the hair
sharp and spiky, the
gaze soft and loving....

we end our day at a
totem (where a whale is be
    coming a wolf), as the
Sun blesses our eyelids

through trees — the memory
of small baskets woven with
rainbow bird feathers that
once loved the Sun, made

by hands that held infants,
cooked food, created beauty,

prepared the dead — Buddha
of a thousand Suns — Buddha

of a thousand universes —
Buddha of infinite possibilities,
like an infant in our arms,
like a whale becoming wolf,

like the shadow of the Earth
seeking fire, we are seeking,
we become....
She who is like the

Sun, for a thousand years,
for a thousand lives, in
this universe or
some other —

I will know
you by the shadow,
the fire of our
Sacred Sun.

To Janine Canan
August 11, 1999, the last
solar eclipse of this millennium —
the healing of the swastika, be
coming ancient, sacred heart of
the Sun for the next 1,000 years....

Sacred Moon

My eighty-three-year-old mother and
I enter the restaurant
slowly — she lifts her
foot at the curb

slowly — she moves to
the bench to wait slowly
slowly — then my name
is called and we begin the

journey to the table oh so
slowly, I hold her hand,
she leans, I have time
to watch the faces — people

in their 40s, 50s, have the
hardest time, this culture
does not honor death, and those
my age feel betrayed by this

proof, this fear of our
temporary bodies — and to
my surprise, some teenagers
smile, shyly, their support

as my eighty-three-year-old mother
and I walk slowly slowly this procession

(the wedding of the body, the spirit) −
this procession of the Sacred Moon,

waxing to crescent to full,
waning full to the
Mystery of the New Moon,
invisible to our eyes −

"Here comes the bride,
here comes the bride...."
I hear the song all around
us as we slowly very

slowly walk to our
table, and though the
sun is bright,
we walk

in the
light
of our
Sacred Moon.

To my mother,
Lydia Villanueva   August 1999

(Dreaming the) Sacred One

Who is the one that listens?
Who is the one that sings?
Who is the one born in darkness?
Who is the one born in light?
Who is the one that feeds the hungry?
Who is the one that kills the innocent?
Who is the one that laughs forever?
Who is the one that weeps forever?
Who is the one that forgets?
Who is the one that remembers?
Who is the one that creates?
Who is the one that destroys?
Who is the beautiful one?
Who is the ugly one?
Who is the wondrous one?
Who is the terrible one?
Who is the dreaming one?
Who is the waking one?
Who is the cherishing one?
Who is the angry one?
Who is the loved one?
Who is the lonely one?
Who is the curious one?
Who is the defeated one?
Who is the dying one?
Who is the undying one?

The Sacred One
who takes our hand
in the singing silence
as we listen to
each other
  US

        To all us humans,
        for the next 1,000 years –

THE SEA

The Sea of Forgiveness

1.

I gather dry, dead moss from
the Ancient Forest, trees so
old they don't remember me —
I tell them who I am

("I am your daughter,
I am your daughter,
born one October fifty-three
years ago, the wind in your

leaves, the wind in your leaves,
I was born, now
I return to you
Ancient Forest of my

Earth.")
I gather dry, dead moss,
my trees,
I gather dry, dead moss.

2.

I gather kindling from
the Ancient Desert, cactus so
old, no memory of me, and
I say to them, I cry

("I am your daughter,
I am your daughter,
born one October fifty-three
years ago, the sun seeking

water, the sun seeking water,
I was born, I was born,
and return to you,
Ancient Desert of my

Earth.")
I gather kindling, spare,
spare kindling, I gather,
my Desert, precious kindling.

3.

I gather fragrant pine, cedar, oak logs
from the Ancient Mountain;
I gather fragrant apple, cherry, pear logs
from the Ancient Valley.

Do you remember me Ancient Mountain?
Do you remember me Ancient Valley?
Perhaps you do, perhaps you do, still
I offer these words, my words

("I am your daughter,
I am your daughter,
born one October fifty-three
years ago, snow on your peaks

for ever, rain seeking roots
for ever, ripening pine, cedar, oak,
apple, cherry, pear and peach;
I was born and return to you,

Ancient Mountain, Ancient Valley, of my Earth.")
I gather fire's wood, Sun's wood, star's wood,
Earth's wood, wood for the ancient cave,
I gather.

4.

I enter the Ancient Cave and she
remembers me, she remembers.
I am silent, no words, no words.
I am silent, silent.

I begin to weep.
I touch Her walls of flesh.
I touch Her walls of living flesh,
blood, bone, heart, womb.

She remembers me. She always remembers.
I place the dry, dead moss in the
center (silently).
I place the spare desert kindling in the

center (silently).
I place the fragrant pine, cedar, oak, apple,
cherry, pear, plum and peach, around the
center (silently).

The darkness is complete
and beautiful.
The darkness is without fear
and beautiful.

Now, I weep with gratitude.

The darkness is without death
and beautiful.
The darkness is without birth
and beautiful. Perfectly beautiful.

I weep with gratitude.

There is only life here, without
end, without beginning.
There is a scent.
Existence gathers, here, in the

center. The Ancient Cave.
I touch Her walls of living
flesh, blood, bone, heart, mind.
I touch Her living, bleeding womb.

I weep with gratitude.

I love this darkness.
I love this scent.
I love the absence of light.
I love Her Womb. Ancient Cave.

Creation.
Before the Sun.
Before the Fire.
Before the Light.

I weep with gratitude.

5.

Days, years, centuries pass.
I gather existence in the
center. Existence has gathered
me. I do not know if

my eyes are open or closed.
I do not know if I'm still dreaming,
century after century, curled up in the
perfect darkness of Creation.

Her scent is mine.
My scent is Hers.
I open my eyes, and still I see
the dream, the wondrous dream of

Creation,
dancing on the living, bleeding walls
of Her flesh, blood, bone, heart, mind,
Her Womb. Her Mystery.

I've become the Dreaming Bear.
I am the Dreaming Bear, and I

dance with the Mystery.
I dream and dance. I dance and dream.

With the Mystery. Creation.
The perfect, beautiful darkness.
For centuries. I do not sing.
I do not weep.

I am the Dreaming Bear
and I dance
and I dream
with the Mystery.

Is this not perfection?
What do I dream?
Voice in the silence.
Some thing singing, flickering.

Fire.

6.

Some thing flutters. Wings.
Butterfly wings. Hummingbird wings.
Wings. Some thing flutters.
Wings. The Eagle. Wings.

The Eagle vomits jewels and
fire, jewels and fire
upon the dry, dead moss,
the spare, precious kindling,

the fragrant logs of the World Tree.
a spark   a wing   a spark   a wing
A SPARK OF FIRE
caught between the beautiful darkness,

caught between my bear hand,
my human hand, my bear hand,
the dream of Creation.
The human asks the bear:

"What did you dream?"

My left hand feeds the Eagle's
fire, my right hand bares its claws
upon the warm cave floor.
The human asks the bear:

"What did you dream?"

7.

Dreaming Bear will know.
I, with words (human, woman)
will say, will sing
the Wisdom Of Bear:

"I dream the Sun, bees, millions
of bees, circling the Sun.
I dream a Rose slowly opening.
I dream the sweetness bees make.

I dream Bear Children, their fur
growing thick for winter.
I dream the far away Stars.
I dream a woman's voice."

(The Woman:)

"The fire is hungry. I watch it
pulse, small heart of the Sun.
The fire is hungry.
I feed it the Earth-fire memories.
I feed it the Sun-fire memories.
I feed it the Star-fire memories.

My childhood of great wonder,
and great terror (I was poor, I was
   hungry, I was loved, I was fed,
   unloved, unfed, caressed and hit;
   I loved to the death, and I fought to
   the death, I did.)

My womanhood of shining wonder, and
her twin, terror (FOUR PERFECT CHILDREN,
   FOUR PERFECT BABIES from my womb,
   my sacred woman's womb —
   each one lived, each one thrived —
   I, the Guardian Of The Gate: These are mine!)

My girlhood and womanhood: the bitterly sweet
   friendship of women (Mothers of my soul, heart,
     mind; without you, no trust: without you, no dreams:
     without you, no poetry, no song,

no wild laughter, no wild tears:
O, my wild women: friends.)

My womanhood of ferocious, tender joys, and
killing, transformative sorrows (The love of
    men, the men I've loved; each one
    a Universe, a Cosmos, a Burning Star;
    each one the nectar, each one the poison;
    and sometimes poison is the cure, I drank.)

My womanhood of empty womb, open hands,
my words in flight (I allowed no man to hit
    me and live. I made love from my own
    deep hunger, fiercely tender. I allowed
    no one to harm my children, ever. If I am
    unloved or loved, know this: I have

never
ever
been
a
slave. Or kept one. You were always free,
my love.

(Dreaming Bear:)

"I dream the Sun, bees, millions
of bees, circling our Sun.
I dream a rose slowly fading.
I dream the root that remembers

the First Rose. I dream I devour the sweetness
that bees make. I dream Bear Children tumbling
into spring, playing with our Sun.
I dream a woman's voice.

"What do you dream?"

8.

(The Woman:)

"My memories rise from the Sacred Fire,
a Rainbow of Butterflies.
They fill the Ancient Cave.
They surround be, completely.

Their wings are soft, soft, with rainbows,
each one perfect, a perfect memory.
How they comfort me with their beauty.
Is this one wonder? Is this one terror?

A rainbow of memories.
A Rainbow of Butterflies.
A rainbow of remembering.
A rainbow of forgetting.

Suddenly, in a swarm, they fly
to the Sea Of Forgiveness, their true
home. Remember this. Know this. Only
freedom can for give.

All my Rainbow Butterflies fly home.
They were never mine.
I was never theirs.
We were dreaming life

together.
Tell me your
dream,
dreaming Bear."

> *To my last blood,*
> *to my wise blood,*
> *the Ancient Cave*
> *Creation.*
>
> *October, Santa Cruz*

Betrayal

(see *reveal:* to make known through divine inspiration)

I search for a bracelet
thrown in the blackberry
bushes years ago, the
bushes now cleared, revealed —

he gave it to me, an easier
gift, rather than his
love — a hummingbird
sits in the setting sun,

blending its green perfectly
with green, only ruby
red betrays it —
I saw a woman at

sunset, walking on the
tide, suddenly she lifted her
shirt exposing her pregnant
miracle to Sun and me —

I am betrayed as
the hummingbird is betrayed,
as the woman is betrayed —
I will never ever find

the bracelet (it was
beautiful, but it wasn't

love) — I am betrayed
by the miracle I see. . . .

my love is a ruby red
mark seeking light —
my love is the child in
the womb seeking warmth —

my love is a child's
morning seeking play —
my love is an elder's
twilight seeking freedom —

my love is the cat's desire,
always seeking birds —
my love is the bird's desire,
always seeking sky —

my love will always
betray me, that I may
know that I may know
what I see....

only the revealed
self
can see, withstand
creation creating itself

before astonished, weary, wondrous
eyes, too stubborn

to close — a human
revealed, betrayed

(by love)

I wear new bracelets.
The hummingbird has a mate.
The woman feels her baby dance.
I am betrayed,

beloved,
by creation
creating itself, for
ever new.   S H I M M E R I N G

November 1999

Stolen Flowers

On my birth day
morning, my 18 year
old son goes for
his 10 mile run,

returns with secret
flowers: marigold, fuschia,
deep purple, light purple,
white iris, deep red bells,

autumn leaves, one red
rose...he places them
in a circle, his
name, a heart, in the

center — once I found such
beauty by chance in rain
and storm, on a picnic
table by the sea,

created lovingly, cunningly,
wisely, innocently . . .
by the magical Fox Of
Childhood, who sings

songs, creates the beauty
we see as children . . .

the wonder. This altar
of wonder, created by

my son who still
hears the magical
Fox Of Childhood —
he gives me

wonder
for my birth
day (these stolen
flowers).

∞ ∞

(To my son, Jules)

I've received many bouquets,
sprays sent with purple ribbons,
two dozen roses with fancy fern

in special vases, delivered
by a stranger who knocked
at my door...but never ever
this priceless message:

your childhood with me —
the tiny one who fit in my hand,
the tall one who gazes down at
me now, the mystery of our

meeting,
mother, son. Our years
of stolen
time –

you remember
I remember
this time.
This (stolen) time.

The healing altar,
your gratitude,
my imperfect love.
The wonder.

October 1999, Santa Cruz

Human Kindness

(Heyoka, Native American "sacred clown")

I met a heyoka at a
gas station in Richmond,
California — he wanted to
clean my windshield, spray

bottle, towels in hand —
at first I said, "No,
thank you," then I
looked into his shiny

eyes and smiled, "Sure."
He was homeless,
he was dirty,
he was unpredictable,

beyond the rules of
daily society —
he was violent,
lonely, and when

he laughed I heard
his rage....sudden noise,
he jumped, "Have ears like a
dog," I think *Vietnam* —

met my eyes briefly,
washed each window

perfectly, paid him more
than promised, gave each other

human kindness, human kindness.

In a checkout line
I remember one more thing,
run to get it, return,
my cart's been moved out of

the way — an elderly
black man with watery
eyes, holding only two
items to my ten or so,

says, "Go on ahead now,"
smiling like the Great Sun
into my face. I refuse
but he won't let me

refuse, puts my cart in
front of his, I thank him,
"Ain't nothin', chile" —
I touch his soft

shoulder, his rainbow
wing (I see it
    tucked away), and
thank him with my own

watery eyes. . . . It's
every thing, this is

every thing, and I know
he knows this, this gift of

human kindness, human kindness.

The women in my class,
in the circle, come
together, bringing pieces
of their lives, their

spirits, glued to card
board, painted circles,
spirals — one woman opens
a box....perfect snake

skin, shiny-dark stone,
poems, one to her father from
a dream, he with wild, beautiful
hair conducting the stars

  (his transformation brings
her grief, this
  joy) — each woman enters
the mystery of her

poetry, vision, each
woman, each woman
shines — one brings the
scent of pears and living

dreams — one shares sacred
crystals in a silver pouch
gathered from desert lakes,
her dreams — one, a dried

wasp's nest (her gathered
   patience) — one, a coyote
dream — one, a dream of
dreaming in dreams —

one with lightning bolts
on her belly and in her
waking dream — and one
brought nothing

but herself, her
self, the nakedness,
the sacredness
of her truth,

her words, her soul,
her tears (our tears)
were the blessing
as laughter is

the blessing, we ended
in laughter, hand in
hand — but she who brought
nothing but her self taught us

human kindness, human kindness. . . .

the true strength and
power of the soul
made real, words dropping
from her lovely mouth,

and each woman gave her
silver, gold, emeralds, pearls,
moonstone, garnet, diamonds,
rubies, onyx, the treasure of

human kindness, human kindness.

Venice Boardwalk, circus
time — fire eater in T-shirt
and thong in December,
warm in the sun, fire

in the mouth jokes, "Used
ta be white fore I started
doin this line a work" —
Japanese tourist holds

cigarette in his mouth
to be lit, I can barely
watch, the fire eater
(wisely) gives up

after three tries, taking
the cigarette from tourist's
mouth, "This man is crazy,"
he says, hugging the

innocent (stupid) tourist.
I walk backwards, gazing
at tattoos on the wall —
the young man who

freshens my almost
twenty year old rose, left
shoulder, adds three lush
green leaves, and one

violet butterfly on my
right ankle (now, I
   feel balanced, left
and right,

forward and backward,
heyokas always do things
backwards)....I see
on his left hand PURA

on his right hand VIDA.
His eyes are kind, generous,
humorous, we speak of his
baby daughter, my grown

children, older than him,
I forget the bee stings
sting sting stinging as we
laugh PURA VIDA

Outside, Jesus wanders in
his robes, blessing every

one in his path — the fire
eater continues his battle

with lighter fluid, his love
of gasps and laughter,
money left in a basket —
lovely women, men, with pierced

every thing, children, every one
skates to hip hop music,
dancing, spinning, playing to
the clicking cameras of

human kindness, human kindness.

As I leave Santa Monica,
the South Land for

the North Land, the
license plate in front of

me says O LOTUS —
I turn to face Time,
I let it devour me,
whole — I can walk at

night with only *night eyes*,
I can run over stones,
my body knows what to do —
I let the night devour

me, whole —
I let the next 1,000
years devour me, whole —
O LOTUS of our

human kindness, human kindness.

December 1999, California
To the next 1,000 years, O lotus....

To the Beautiful Soul of Men

Last night on 60 Minutes
I saw Denzel Washington
speak of his life,
being born black

in this time, the women
that saved him, the mother
he loves. His eyes aren't
those of handsome, arrogant

(mostly) white men who pretend
to know something you don't know —
this man knows.
He's journeyed through self

hatred, rage and folly
to his wisdom — this
is the kind of man
Toni Morrison says,

"Women weep when he enters
a room" — it's true,
I couldn't help it,
sitting on my black

leather couch in Santa Cruz,
California, watching 60 Minutes,
his face on my flat
TV screen, I wept,

tears streaming down my
feminist face, that such
wholeness, grace, wisdom,
strength, real feeling (rage

and tenderness) is housed
in the beautiful body of
this man, in the beautiful
soul of this man.

Most men hide this, train
it out of themselves (by
self, father, patriarchal
culture) — so, I just wept

for what I've seen in my
own sons, those rare men
strong enough to keep it,
nurture it,

treasure it
in self and other.
The beautiful soul of men.
Makes grown women weep

with longing,
with burned-out grief
and burned-out rage.
And living, burning joy.

January 2000

January 1, 2000

Dear World,

Early in the morning, the
31st of December, I turn
on PBS to see you,
dear World, edge into

your new self, new
year, new century,
new millennium — the first
thing I see is a Karmic

Ritual from Bali —
dark cave lit by
fire, corpse on one
side, skeleton on

the other, feast in
the center — then, the
dancers, one beautiful woman,
two beautiful men — they

dance the corpse to
life, especially the beautiful
young woman — she dances
calmly, very calmly, every

gesture aimed with magic —
the corpse startles to
life, groans with choice,
this life, he is amazed

to be born again,
to be here again,
he's forgotten how to
breathe, to eat, to

desire any thing —
the beautiful woman
dances calmly, so calmly,
her beauty guiding appetites —

mother, sister, lover, wife,
womb and cave, the fire —
he re members desire
so well he goes slightly mad

with it, wasting breath,
wasting food, wasting time,
the karmic wheel turns,
he screeches with raw

desire, the beautiful woman
dances calmly, oh so calmly,
aiming Her Magic to each One
lucky to be born,

to be born and
born again (burning karma

   burning karma), loving
the other, killing the other

(burning karma burning karma)
until we honor She who is
never born, never dies,
but dances. So calmly.

   ෆ ෨

Burning karma, burning karma,
we enter a new age,
century, millennium — we've
seen The Dancer,

 dear World,
dance our
burning karma
so calmly. Into peace.

Earth aligned to the center of our galaxy, the Milky Way, on December 21, 1999, a celestial event that occurs once every 26,000 years — and on December 21, 2012, the Solstice Sun will align with the center of the Milky Way, a celestial event that takes place once every 26,000 years. This is also the date on which the Great Cycle of the Mayan Long Count calendar ends. Mayan astronomers foretold that this date marks a time when human intelligence, spirit, will begin a new and creative age, the Unfolding.

Desire

The God
caresses
the Goddess
with a small

white snake, then
puts it in a pouch to sleep —
the Goddess sets it
free.

Dream, May 1999

About the Author

B*orn and raised* in the San Francisco Mission District, Alma Luz Villanueva is of Yaqui, Spanish, and German ancestry. Her first book of poetry, *Bloodroot* (1977), attracted considerable critical attention. That same year, her manuscript entitled simply "Poems" won the Third Annual Chicano Literary Prize at the University of California at Irvine.

Villanueva's autobiographical poem, *Mother, May I?* (1978), which was long her best-known work, fictionalizes through personalized myth the cyclic changes in a woman's life and the joyous emergence into wholeness.

Her first novel, *The Ultraviolet Sky* (1988), received the American Book Award of the Before Columbus Foundation. It was reissued by Anchor Doubleday. Her second novel, *Naked Ladies* (1994), received the PEN Oakland Josephine Miles Award. Villanueva's latest novel is *Luna's California Poppies* (2001).

Other poetry collections include *La Chingada* (1985), an epic poem published in English and Spanish, *Life Span* (1984), and *Planet* (1993). *Planet*, which won the Latin American Writers Institute Award in poetry (1994, New York), explores racism, sexual abuse, and poverty. Prior to *Vida*, Villanueva's latest collection of poetry was *Desire* (1998). She is also the author of a collectionof short fiction, *Weeping Woman: La Llorona and Other Stories* (1994).

Villanueva, who holds a MFA in Creative Writing from Vermont College at Norwich University, teaches in the low-residency MFA creative writing program at Antioch University, Los Angeles. Villanueva also travels during the year to give readings and teach workshops all over the globe. Currently she is living in Santa Fe, New Mexico, and writing.

Colophon

Seven hundred and fifty copies of the first edition of *Vida*, by Alma Luz Villanueva, have been printed on 70 pound natural linen paper, containing fifty percent recycled fiber, by Williams Printing & Graphics of San Antonio, Texas. The book title is set in Bickley Script. Text and interior titles were set in a contemporary version of Classic Bodoni., originally designed by the 18th century Italian typographer and punchcutter, Giambattista Bodoni, press director for the Duke of Parma.

The first fifty copies of *Vida* have been specially bound, and were numbered and signed by the author. This book was entirely designed and produced by Bryce Milligan, publisher, Wings Press.

Wings Press was founded in 1975 by J. Whitebird and Joseph F. Lomax as "an informal association of artists and cultural mythologists dedicated to the preservation of the literature of the nation of Texas." The publisher/editor since 1995, Bryce Milligan is honored to carry on and expand that mission to include the finest in American writing.

2991

Other recent and forthcoming
literature from Wings Press

Way of Whiteness by Wendy Barker (2000)

Hook & Bloodline by Chip Dameron (2000)

Splintered Silences by Greta de León (2000)

Incognito: A Secret Jew's Journey by María Espinosa (Spring 2002)

Peace in the Corazón by Victoria García-Zapata (1999)

Street of Seven Angels by John Howard Griffin (Spring 2002)

Cande, te estoy llamando by Celeste Guzmán (1999)

Winter Poems from Eagle Pond by Donald Hall (1999)

Initiations in the Abyss by Jim Harter (Fall 2001)

Strong Box Heart by Sheila Sánchez Hatch (2000)

Patterns of Illusion by James Hoggard (Spring 2002)

This Side of Skin by Deborah Paredez (Spring 2002)

Fishlight: A Dream of Childhood by Cecile Pineda (Fall 2001)

The Love Queen of the Amazon by Cecile Pineda (Fall 2001)

Mama Yetta and Other Poems by Hermine Pinson (1999)

Smolt by Nicole Pollentier (1999)

Garabato Poems by Virgil Suárez (1999)

Sonnets to Human Beings by Carmen Tafolla (1999)

Sonnets and Salsa by Carmen Tafolla (Fall 2001))

The Laughter of Doves by Frances Marie Treviño (Fall 2001)

Finding Peaches in the Desert by Pam Uschuk (2000)

One Legged Dancer by Pam Uschuk (Spring 2002)

Vida by Alma Luz Villanueva (Fall 2001)

AEE-5186